GILLIAN HIGGINS

MINDFULNESS
AT WORK AND HOME

A SIMPLE GUIDE

PRAISE FOR *MINDFULNESS AT WORK AND HOME*

'This book is an excellent introduction to mindfulness for all who find the pressure of work or home life stressful. As an international criminal barrister, Gillian Higgins knows first-hand how overwhelming such pressure can be. In this book, written with genuine warmth, openness and clarity, she stays close to the scientific evidence, as well as drawing from her own experience of practicing and teaching mindfulness, to offer simple and practical steps to stay well in the midst of the stresses of life. I warmly commend this book.'

Mark Williams, Emeritus Professor of Clinical Psychology, University of Oxford

'*Mindfulness at Work and Home* demystifies how to practice mindfulness in today's ever-intensifying world. Higgins weaves the science of neuroplasticity and her own courageous transformation into an accessible guide with grounding meditations, actionable steps, and kind encouragement for meditators of all experience. This book is for those living in the real world looking for focus, compassion, and authenticity in our commute, communication, and all the moments in between.'

Sharon Salzberg, author of *Lovingkindness* and *Real Happiness*

'International criminal barrister, Gillian Higgins, has written a comprehensive guide to the benefits of mindfulness meditation for both work and home. She tells us about the profound difference mindfulness has made to her life and gives us a roadmap to discovering what it can do for us. I wholeheartedly recommend this book to you.'

Mary Pearson, CEO and co-founder of the British School of Meditation and author of *Meditation, The Stress Solution*

'Mindfulness restores the soul. In these uncertain times, Gillian Higgins provides a path for gaining insight as to who we are, what we are doing and what we should be doing. This book adds meaning to our lives.'

Steven Kay QC, International Barrister

'Gilly is the "Queen of Calm". Her approach makes life better. I want to buy this book for everyone I know ... and make them read it!'

nda Gore Browne, writer, cook, mother and finalist on the first series of *The British Bake Off*

'The work of a barrister is demanding and pressured and can be very lonely. The stress under which they work is often transmitted to their clerks who are there to support them. Only another barrister can really understand the stresses and strains of life at or around the Bar. Gillian Higgins is uniquely placed to open the "mindfulness closet" and to encourage an inherently reluctant audience to embrace the practice of mindfulness.

Coming from a place of knowledge, this practical handbook demonstrates the benefits of mindfulness and provides the reader with a step-by-step guide on how to introduce and incorporate mindfulness into the day-to-day schedule. The background and traits of barristers often result in having a number of the characteristics that this book will help to calm: stress, distorted thinking, a busy mind and managing conflict to name a few. This is an excellent, practical book and is exactly what is needed.'

Carolyn McCombe, Head of Professional Standards and ADR at 4 Pump Court and Nick Hill, Senior Clerk at 3 New Square and former Chair of the Institute of Barristers' Clerks

'Gillian Higgins gives us the science and the benefits of mindfulness meditation and, best of all, really simple tools and techniques for use in our everyday lives. Gillian addresses common questions like, "I don't have enough time to meditate", "how to deal with your inner critical voice" and "dealing with difficult colleagues". Practical, relevant and achievable.'

General Counsel at FTSE 100 Company

'This is an engaging and practical guide to mindfulness and sets out how easy it is to incorporate into your daily life at work and home. You may think you are too busy to practice mindfulness or may have some doubts about its benefits, but in this book Gillian will persuade you how mindfulness can transform your life – bringing greater clarity, focus, calm and better relationships with the people around you. In the 21st century hyper-connected world of information overload, this book is a must!'

Eizabeth Rimmer, Chief Executive of LawCare

The right of Gillian Higgins to be identified as author of this Work
has been asserted by her in accordance with sections 77 and 78 of
the Copyright, Designs and Patents Act 1988

ISBN 978-1-910453-80-3

This book is not intended as a substitute for the medical advice
of physicians. The reader should regularly consult a physician in
matters relating to his/her health and particularly with respect to any
symptoms that may require diagnosis or medical attention

A CIP catalogue record for this book is available from
the British Library

Cover design: ironicitalics.com

Typesetting: Sheerdesignandtypesetting.co.uk

Printed and bound in BZGraf S.A.

To my family

CONTENTS

PREFACE

The world can be a noisy place. There are constant demands, nagging complaints, frequent requests and decisions to be made. There is too little distance between comfort and fear, between action and anger. Technology is setting the pace – and we are struggling to keep up. It all feels a bit too tense. We need time out, a moment to breathe and space to reflect.

Working in different countries around the world, I have spent a significant part of the last two decades making decisions, meeting deadlines, giving difficult advice and managing teams. As an international criminal lawyer, I have represented heads of state, former presidents, military leaders and politicians. In the process, I've analysed corridors of evidence of war crimes, crimes against humanity and genocide. It has been a unique experience, but it has also involved prolonged periods of stress, which have periodically spilled over into my private life.

However, it wasn't until I was about to become a parent for the first time that I really started to think about how I wanted to feel less worried and more present. I wanted to be able to respond more sensitively to situations at work and home. I wasn't sure how to bring about these changes but I knew from my limited experience of meditation some years ago, that it had helped me to feel a sense of calm. Over the past few years, interest in mindfulness had grown significantly and I was keen to learn more. I joined a local class, read as many books as I could and started to practise at home, even when I didn't want to.

After a few months, I started to feel a subtle difference. At work I became more able to cope with stressful situations, less reactively. I interpreted the outcomes of difficult conversations less personally and found rejection and disappointment somehow easier to handle. It was hard to explain this to others, but I felt slight positive shifts in my ability to manage people and difficult conversations. It even made my commute to London more manageable as it became a time of practice, rather than a source of irritation. The benefits were real. I managed to avoid or stop arguments at home by becoming aware of the tone of my voice – and changing it slightly. I paused and breathed deeply before responding to the inexplicable rage of my young daughter. I became aware of the physical rising of my own anger and frustration when things went wrong. I discerned more readily when to rest rather than 'push on through' and became more compassionate towards myself when I didn't live up to my own high expectations.

With time, I became a better listener, less insistent on being heard or being right. I started to distinguish more clearly between the battles worth fighting and those that deserved no response at all. I said 'no' more often, streamlined priorities, decluttered my office and sold possessions. Slowly it started to change how I responded to the inevitable ups and downs of daily life. It allowed me to repair and restore relations much more quickly when things went sideways.

As a new parent, I got better at carving out much-needed breathing space and enjoying the moment, *whatever* it ended up looking like. I was able to drop, or at least amend, unrealistic expectations of how it was to raise a child. I used mindfulness to bring a moment of calm to the busyness of the school run, the chaos of play dates and the challenge of connecting with new parents without judgment.

I could choose to breathe and refrain from losing my temper when my daughter threw yet another tantrum, and saw the wisdom of bringing her in close. I was able to decide whether to react to her emotional outbursts or simply let them pass. When our family Christmas lunch ended up with my daughter crying under the table, rather than sat in her seat, I had the know-how to be able to drop the judgment of *how Christmas should be* and accept how it was – warts and all. Mindfulness helped me to manage the moment with less resistance and more resilience. It also strengthened my relationships with family, friends and work colleagues as I became slower to judge and quicker to mend. While I didn't necessarily become visibly calmer, I began to recognise when I was at risk of being hijacked by an overwhelming emotion. Practising mindfulness empowered me to pause long enough to decide whether to be washed away by the emotion or allow it to wash over me, knowing that it would move on, if I let it.

After several years, I decided to train to teach mindfulness meditation. I felt passionately that I wanted to be able to share it with my own professional colleagues. This was at a time when the Bar was only just starting to recognise the importance of well-being. In a profession where *we eat what we kill*, it wasn't easy to admit to those around me that I spent time meditating – and moreover, that it kept me sane – most of the time. It took me at least six months to come out of the *mindfulness closet*, which I'm told by more senior practitioners is no time at all. I had wondered how colleagues would perceive me when I explained my practice. Perhaps they would view it as an inability to cope or that somehow I needed a crutch. While I didn't grow up in a tepee, I wondered whether I might be perceived as 'new-age', 'alternative' or somehow less trustworthy. Might it be a point of separation between us, rather than a meeting of 'well-being' minds?

In fact, what I found was that once I started to share my experience with others, colleagues took time to talk about the pressures they were under. The door opened to many difficult conversations on topics that at that time were rarely spoken about at the Bar.

After approaching Gray's Inn, one of the four professional associations for barristers, I was invited to hold a series of mindfulness sessions. The response was both unexpected and encouraging. Each week, twenty-five suit-clad barristers of different levels of seniority would come along, drop their bags and sit in a circle to practise mindfulness meditation. Each week, they returned. When *The Evening Standard* newspaper carried an article about a war crimes barrister holding meditation classes, the word spread and others joined. The sessions continued in my chambers' main conference room and numbers grew steadily, largely by word-of-mouth.

As I suspected at the outset, we are a reluctant profession when it comes to opening up about our own well-being, but slowly, things are changing. In this book, my aim is to showcase the simplicity of mindfulness and how it can be used to great effect by *anyone, anywhere and everywhere*. Each chapter contains guidance on the practice of mindfulness, answers frequently asked questions, and tackles key themes, such as how mindfulness can help to reduce stress, tame your inner critical voice, improve sleep, increase focus and reduce anxiety. There are tips, hints and practical suggestions on how to incorporate mindfulness into your daily routine. Each chapter contains a guided meditation with explanatory notes. A fourteen-day journal has also been included for you to record your experience.

I hope this guide will demonstrate how easily you can get started in order to reap the benefits in a way that works for you.

Finally, I owe a deep debt of gratitude to all my mentors, teachers, friends, family and colleagues who have helped me along the way. Thank you.

CHAPTER 1

GETTING STARTLᴊ

WHAT IS MINDFULNESS?

Mindfulness has been practised for thousands of years, and many people have heard about it – but what exactly is it? Mindfulness is paying attention to moments of everyday life with curiosity and openness, on purpose. It involves dropping into your present moment experience and being aware of what you're doing, while you're doing it, with a non-judgmental attitude. In essence, it's about experiencing the 'here and now', rather than hankering after how you would like life to be. Mindfulness involves bringing awareness to present thoughts, emotions and sensations in your body, as well as what is going on externally – such as sights and sounds, touch and smell.

It might sound surprising, but we spend almost half of the time anywhere but in the present moment. Research shows that the mind wanders on average 46.9 per cent of the time throughout the day, and that a wandering mind is an unhappy mind.[1] Even when you desperately want to be immersed in what you're doing, for example taking part in a celebration, helping a colleague or playing with a small child, your mind is often elsewhere, dwelling in the past or floating ahead to the future. The problem with being 'elsewhere' is that the brain has a negativity bias, so it is often drawn to experiences that create discomfort or pain.

By practising mindfulness, you become aware of your present experience and your mind is able to capture the snapshot of the moment, before it's gone. It also helps you to befriend your mind and notice when it wanders. It's a practice that trains you to observe your thoughts as they arise, without over-analysing or over-identifying with them. It puts you, rather than your thoughts, in the driving seat, and prevents a rush to judgment. It invites you to approach life with an attitude of gentle curiosity and kindness towards yourself.

Mindfulness also empowers you to turn towards difficult emotions. With a mindful approach, you don't reject or deny powerful feelings, which may be justified and strongly felt. Instead, you become aware of their emotional pull and get to decide how best to respond. It also involves the realisation that the present moment is all that there is, and while you may not be able to change a situation, you can mindfully adapt your response towards it.

'What would it be like if I could accept life – accept this moment – exactly as it is?'

Tara Brach

You can practise mindfulness in different ways. One way is to learn mindfulness meditation, which involves paying attention to your moment-to-moment experience with acceptance, patience and kindness to yourself. This formal practice is discussed in greater detail overleaf.

Another way is to use what I call 'daily mindfulness practices'. These are instances where you pause, breathe and bring moment-to-moment awareness to an aspect of your everyday life, such as the brewing of your tea or the taking of your morning shower. By pausing in this way, you might notice the aroma of your drink or the sensation of the water as you take in your experience fully. So often, the uniqueness of the moment is lost as we slip into automatic pilot mode, focusing on simply getting through the day.

Daily mindfulness practices can also be times where you bring a *mindful attitude* to an aspect of your work or home life. You could for example, bring patience, kindness or curiosity to the way you communicate, set a positive intention for the day or conduct a meeting.

Mindfulness involves a different way of *being*, as opposed to *doing*. It encourages you to notice life as it unfolds, so that you don't miss what's going on, while you're busy being elsewhere.

WHAT IS MINDFULNESS MEDITATION?

It is generally accepted that there are three common forms of mindfulness meditation: **focused-attention, open-monitoring** and **loving kindness (compassion) meditation**.

In **focused-attention meditation**, you use a point of focus, such as the breath, a mantra (a short phrase such as 'Breathing in, I feel peace; breathing out I am calm'), the sound of a bell chiming, the smell of a flower, the flame of a candle or sensations arising in your body. When your mind wanders away from the point of focus, or 'anchor' as it is sometimes called, you notice where the mind has wandered to and gently guide it back to its focal point. During your practice, the aim is to return to your present experience, time and time again, without judgment. This type of meditation helps to develop the capacity to remain focused while also being alert to distractions as they arise. You start to recognise that thoughts are not facts about you and that they come and go of their own accord, if you allow them to do so. The practice teaches you that you have a choice whether or not to act upon them, and how best to respond. It reminds you that a habitual knee-jerk reaction is not your only option.

> 'Life is available only in the present moment.'
>
> Thich Nhat Hanh

With mindfulness, you don't have to believe the early morning anxious voice forecasting that your speech will not go well. You have a choice whether or not to snap at your child when he or she refuses to get dressed, and you can override your irritation towards your partner who has forgotten to put out the dustbin. With practice, you might find that daily frustrations reduce in number as you adopt an attitude of mindfulness.

In **open-monitoring meditation**, you observe things as they arise and come into your awareness, without having any particular point of focus. You watch what arrives in a detached manner, whether it's internal thoughts, emotions or your physical surroundings, both pleasant and unpleasant. When your mind wanders, you gently bring it back to openly monitoring the moment as you find it. You refrain from latching on and getting carried away by powerful distractions. This practice helps to cultivate a less reactive awareness towards emotions, thoughts and sensations. It's akin to watching a scene from a film or actors on the stage. It encourages us to detach from any one particular thought, feeling or response – and observe the scene as it plays out, without trying to control the outcome.

Loving kindness (compassion) meditation focuses on developing feelings of goodwill, compassion and understanding towards others. During a meditation, you might repeat compassionate wishes for the well-being of others and yourself. Phrases such as 'May I be happy', 'May I be healthy', 'May I be safe', 'May I live my life with ease' are used as a focus of attention during the meditation. Practising loving kindness helps to develop compassion for others, reduce anxiety and increase feelings of social connectedness. It also helps you to be kinder to yourself, an attitude that doesn't always come naturally.

Mindfulness meditation isn't complicated, exclusive or long-winded, and can be practised by anyone, anywhere. You can use it at home, in a meeting, at a family gathering, on the train, at bedtime or even after grappling with a difficult piece of work or an irritable child. Its beauty is its sheer versatility and portability. Importantly, it doesn't require you to stop your thoughts or empty your mind, which is a common misconception. Instead, the practice is centred around developing your awareness, quietening the mind and training your ability to pay attention. It is simple and scientifically verifiable. Over time, you gain a better understanding of how your mind works, its weaknesses, vulnerabilities and where it likes to wander, which can often be a revelation in itself.

GETTING STARTED

When I started to meditate, I was inundated with feelings of frustration and uncertainty as to whether or not I was doing it right. The time seemed to move incredibly slowly and I would often fall asleep before the guided meditation had ended.

It's worth remembering that we each bring our unique experience to the practice of mindfulness meditation. You may be a complete beginner or you may have tried to meditate in the past but lost the motivation to continue. Perhaps you think you won't be able to find the time or be any good at it? Or maybe you believe it's only for certain types of people, or that by meditating you will somehow lose your edge? All of these feelings are entirely normal.

This chapter addresses commonly asked questions about mindfulness meditation, how to get started and how to tackle some of the initial challenges you may face in the days, weeks and months ahead.

INTENTION AND MOTIVATION

The prospect of kick-starting any new habit often feels daunting, no matter what the benefits may be. Right now, it may seem like an insurmountable challenge to find even five or ten minutes for yourself, every day. But when you think about, it isn't long. You just need to prioritise the time so that it becomes part of your daily routine, just like brushing your teeth – it's as simple as that.

At the outset, it's worth considering your intention, motivation to practice and how you are going to prioritise your mindful minutes.

> **Tip**
>
> It's worth remembering that you don't have to like meditating. Choose to do it anyway, with kindness to yourself. Notice any subtle changes in your behaviour and how you feel.

I remember my first meditation teacher asking me what had brought me to her class. She asked what I hoped to achieve and whether I was prepared to practise, even when I didn't feel like it. I remember reflecting on these questions, uncertain of the answers. I knew that I wanted to reap some of the well-known benefits of mindfulness, but I wasn't sure how I would find the time to do it. She advised me to approach it with a patient attitude and a gentle perseverance, advice that resonated and encouraged me to keep going. Acceptance of the challenges you face and an attitude of non-striving towards any particular goal will stand you in good stead. Thankfully, unlike many other areas of life, mindfulness is non-competitive, so you can always begin again, at any time, whenever you need to, without repercussion or a sense of failure.

'A child knows the value
of being in the present.
Actually a child has no definite
idea of the past or the future.
His or her happiness resides in the
present ... For a child, a day is a
day and it never returns.'

Ken Mogi

It's useful to approach your practice with what's known as a 'beginner's mind' – an attitude of openness, of curiosity and a real sense of kindness to yourself. While everyone starts out in life with this attitude, the mind tends to take over and calls up memories, expectations and even fears when it recognises a situation, thinking, 'I know how this is.' These preconceptions often prevent you from connecting with what's really going on.

Having a beginner's mind doesn't mean that you become forgetful of lessons you have already learned, but rather that you look at things in a fresh light, as if for the first time. The spider's web along your path, the architectural beauty of a building, the timid deer at dusk in the railway car park, or the devastating clarity of the sky at night are all there to be seen anew. Bringing this attitude to your mindfulness practice helps you to approach your present-moment experience, fully alive to its uniqueness.

It's normal, however, at times to feel resistant to practising and to make any excuse not to meditate. However, in my experience, these are the times when you stand to benefit the most. So when you feel reluctant, resentful or even uninspired, see if you can take a moment to consider why you want to bring more mindfulness into your life. Perhaps it's to cope with stress, to sleep better or to improve your productivity at work. Recognising your natural resistance and recalling your personal motivation will help you to stay committed to developing your practice on a daily basis – no matter what.

POSITION AND POSTURE

Before you start meditating, you'll want to spend a few moments settling in. I take the view that you can meditate in any position – sitting, lying down or walking. Your posture should be comfortable, balanced and alert, with your spine straight but neither strained, nor slumped.

If you prefer to sit, you may want to use a high-backed chair or a supportive meditation cushion on the floor. Uncross your legs and let your arms rest by your sides with your hands on your thighs or in your lap, palms facing down.

If you choose to lie down, find somewhere comfortable, again with your hands resting by your sides, and your legs uncrossed. If you meditate on your bed, be aware of the natural temptation to drift off to sleep. If this happens, reassure yourself with the fact that you were meditating up until the moment you dropped off and that it's just a sign that you need more rest.

Close your eyes, or if you prefer, keep them open, lowering your gaze to a point in front of you. Release your jaw and shoulders. If you need to adjust your posture at any time during the meditation, my advice is to take a moment to do so, without berating or judging yourself. Often during a meditation practice, when you sit or lie still for any length of time, you become aware of aches, pains or sensations arising in your body. If this happens, notice your experience and breathe gently into these areas, using it as a rare moment to check in with what's going on inside you.

WHAT DO I NEED?

I'm often asked, 'What should I wear?' and, 'Do I need any special equipment?' The simple answer is that all you need is your body and your breath. You can meditate in your pyjamas or your suit – any outfit will do. There's no need to wear special clothes, light candles, sit on the floor or invest in a new meditation cushion.

One of the beauties of mindfulness is its flexibility. You can practise anywhere, just as you are – at work or at home. Most of the time, those around you won't even know that you're meditating.

Tip

When you start your mindfulness practice, try not to be too critical of yourself – a little every day goes a long way. If several days pass without practice, just gently start again and see how you can make it work for you.

I keep a cushion on the floor in my office at home, which reminds me that all I need to do is to sit on it at some point during the day – the rest will come naturally. I use a clock or a fifteen-minute hourglass to notice how long I've been sitting, if I feel the urge to check. Generally, the longer I sit, the longer I want to sit, as it feels like a welcome break. With practice, you even start to become mindful of when you're not mindful – which acts as a gentle reminder to step out of automatic pilot mode, for at least part of the day, and experience what's actually going on inside and around you.

WHERE AND WHEN TO MEDITATE

When deciding where to meditate, it's helpful to use the same space every time if you can, to support the building of your new practice. Try to find a place where you will not be disturbed, even if it's just for a few minutes. This may be the bedroom, the office, a spare room, the garden shed or even the car at the start or end of a journey. You might find that you can meditate on the bus or the train into work, even if the circumstances aren't perfect. If background noises arise, practise letting them go in the same way that you let go of thoughts or sensations.

Many people find it useful to meditate at the start of the day when they feel alert and rested. Others prefer to practise before going to bed. Ultimately, it's about getting into a routine and finding a time that works for you. There's no right way or only way to meditate. If I haven't meditated for a couple of days, I often hear the words

Tip

Are you able to use your commute to listen to a short guided meditation or read an article on the benefits of practising mindfulness to support your motivation? Consider how to make your mindfulness a natural part of your daily routine.

of the American mindfulness teacher Dr Jon Kabat-Zinn sounding in my ears, reminding me to practise as though my life depends on it — which in many ways, it does. Whenever I stop for any length of time, I notice I have less patience, feel less generous towards others (and myself) and am more easily irritated. These shifts remind me that I need to carve out the time to meditate.

HOW LONG?

When you start to meditate, the best advice is to take small steps. At the beginning, it can be a real challenge to find the time. See if you can meditate for just a few minutes every day. You could do this by listening to one of the short guided meditations in this book. Alternatively, start by trying one or two of the daily mindfulness practices that resonate with you. Perhaps take a pause before you start to drive, hit the keyboard or enter your workplace.

While there are no set rules, the more you practise mindfulness meditation, the more profound and lasting the benefits

'Meditation is the ultimate mobile device; you can use it anywhere, anytime, unobtrusively.'

Sharon Salzberg

will be.[2] In the first few months, it's often recommended to aim for ten to fifteen minutes, four or five times a week, as you build up to a daily practice. However, even just a few minutes every day can start to steer your thoughts and responses in a mindful direction.

Cultivating mindfulness helps you to take situations less personally and leave the often-concocted drama of the moment to one side. In the workplace, you might find yourself becoming less attached to particular outcomes, more balanced in your response, and better able to add value to the resolution of problems that arise. In practical terms, you may decide to leave the room, rather than explode with anger; save an email to draft, rather than fire it off; or have a conversation with a colleague over coffee the following day, rather than share your strong views immediately. While we can't control the rise and fall of our emotions, we can start to learn how to modify our response.

THE TRAVELLING MIND

It's good to know at the outset that it's normal for the mind to wander when you meditate. The mind moves quickly into 'doing' mode, for example thinking, planning or worrying, skipping from one thought to another. It's often unsettled, restless and indecisive.

Within seconds, you may find yourself flitting between worrying about a work deadline to planning your child's birthday party, to regretting an argument with a friend, to wishing you lived somewhere else, with someone else. A day of mind-wandering can leave you feeling overwhelmed, exhausted and somewhat depleted, often with no solution in sight.

> **Tip**
>
> At the end of your meditation practice, see if you can recall where the mind wandered to and perhaps write it down. It's often helpful to identify its preoccupations by using these insights. In this way, you start to befriend your mind and learn more about its behaviour and habits.

Mindfulness meditation enables the mind to steady itself and stray less often. Researchers at the University of California found that even an eight-minute instruction of mindfulness lessens the extent to which the mind wanders.[3] The same researchers also found that just two weeks of mindfulness training improved concentration and working memory.

So, if you find yourself getting frustrated or even angry when your mind starts to wander, reassure yourself that it's perfectly normal. As your ability to concentrate strengthens, your wandering thoughts will reduce in number. See if you can allow the thoughts or sensations that do arise to pass as quickly as they appeared, and simply begin again, by following one breath, and then another. No judgment or criticism – just an acknowledgement of your experience as it is.

'Our mind wanders mostly to something about ourselves – my thoughts, my emotions, my relationships, who liked my new post on my Facebook page – all the minutiae of our life story... because the self ruminates on what's bothering us, we feel relieved when we can turn it off.'

Goleman & Davidson

DAILY MINDFULNESS

At the end of each chapter, this section contains suggestions on how to incorporate mindfulness into your daily life at work and home.

This chapter focuses on how to incorporate a mindful pause and how to reclaim your commute. There's also guidance on using mindfulness when you brew your tea or coffee and how the practice of gratitude can positively impact your day.

WORKPLACE

The Mindful Pause

Setting aside time to meditate daily can be hard to accomplish when you're confronted with thoughts about what else you should or could be doing, particularly when you're at work.

The Mindful Pause is a simple and effective way of bringing mindfulness into the workplace and the home. It involves finding time during the day to pause, breathe, notice your experience and then return to the task in hand. It's not a moment of no activity, or an immediate escape from the chaos that may surround you. Rather, it's an intentional interruption to the flow of what you're doing, wherever you are. It allows you to step outside your train of thought and is an opportunity for you to reset your mind, notice what's new and consider how you want to respond. It can be a game-changer in terms of helping to relieve stress and reduce tension.

The Practice: To introduce the Mindful Pause into your working day, consciously follow the passage of your in-breath and out-breath, wherever you are. Notice what arises and when your mind starts to wander into planning, worrying or thinking mode, gently guide it back to following the passage of your breath for a few moments.

'Let it be
a contrast to
being all caught up.
Let it be like popping
a bubble. Let it be just
a moment in time, and
then go on.'

Pema Chödrön

When you pause, be patient and curious about your experience. See if you can integrate several intentional mindful pauses throughout your day, to foster more presence. You might consider inserting a mindful standing pause before going into a meeting, or before delivering a presentation. You might even pause before you start your work for the day. If it helps, note down the pauses you take, how they make you feel, and see if you notice any benefits. It's a portable, simple practice that you can do at any given moment.

WORKPLACE

The Commute

I often use my commute to London by train as an opportunity to meditate. No one knows I am doing it and as I let thoughts, sensations and sounds come and go, I'm reminded that I can practise even in the busiest, most cramped or noisiest of conditions.

I am fascinated by the extent to which people use their electronic devices when commuting. My train research shows that eight out of ten of those who commute on my train line are 'attached to distraction', with some being attached to more than one device at once! While some use their device to catch up on work, others are merely scrolling or zoning out. So how could you spend this time more mindfully if you're one of the many thousands who commute to work on a daily basis? Could you transform your journey using mindfulness and boost your energy, ready for the day ahead?

The Practice: Choose to give yourself a break from attachment to distraction by seeing if for at least five or ten minutes you can turn off your phone, iPad, laptop – and simply be. Close your eyes or lower your gaze. Let go of any thoughts that arise and return to your breath, using it as your anchor or point of focus. Now start to direct your attention to different parts of your body. Perhaps start with your feet and slowly move to the top of your head – taking in your whole body breathing. Notice any sensations that arise. You might feel a sense of warmth, a tingling, an ache or nothing at all. After a few minutes, open your eyes. See how you feel after this short period of letting go.

HOME

The Tea or Coffee Practice

How often have you gone to make yourself a drink only to be distracted by doing several things at the same time? Do you re-boil the kettle or even walk away forgetting to make the drink, with other thoughts on your mind? Rather than seeing mindfulness as another thing to add to your 'To Do' list, try using this practice to recharge your batteries when you make your next cup of tea or coffee.

The Practice: When you boil the kettle or turn on the coffee machine, take a moment to pause, breathe deeply and stay with the process. Refrain from doing anything else at the same time. Wait for the kettle to boil or the coffee to brew. See if you can let go of any thoughts that come into your mind, sensing your feet planted firmly on the ground. Once you've made your drink, take a moment to smell the aroma, feel the texture of the cup, sense the heat and watch the steam rise. Sit with your drink for a few moments until you take your first sip. Use this time to continue to follow your breath. Notice how it feels to be present, rather than distracted or elsewhere.

HOME

Feeling Gratitude

The brain's negativity bias means that you're more likely to dwell on something that has gone wrong, than to celebrate or soak up a moment of success. Too much negativity, however, can lead to unhealthy ways of thinking. Research shows that practising gratitude, being thankful for the good things in your life, is a great antidote to negative emotions. Studies show that gratitude is a powerful tool for strengthening relationships and building optimism. Expressing your thanks can also improve your overall sense of well-being.

The Practice: Actively practising gratitude makes you feel better and it can have a positive impact on your creativity, health, relationships and the quality of your work. Taking a moment to be grateful helps condition your mind for positivity and can even improve your sleep.[4] So consider what you could be thankful for today, however small. It might be that you're grateful for the roof over your head, your job, the weather, your children, food or love. See if you can get into the habit of recording your gratitude over the next two weeks and notice how this practice makes you feel. Use the mindfulness and gratitude log at the back of this book if it helps.

'Counting our blessings has a huge impact upon our lives. So few of us realise this and so many of us become immersed in complaining about life, our job, the state of our home, our partner, even our Internet connection. The positive state and increased personal energy that gratitude brings helps us to approach situations like these in a more positive, optimistic, confident and direct way.'

David Hamilton

* MINDFULNESS MEDITATION *

At the end of each chapter there is a guided meditation for you to listen to at any time of the day or night. The six meditations are available for download from the Practical Meditation website at

www.practicalmeditation.co.uk/podcasts

Conscious Breathing Meditation

In this three-minute practice, use the counting of your breath as an anchor to the present moment. Consider your intention, motivation and posture, setting aside a few minutes in a quiet space to listen to the conscious breathing meditation.

A QUICK REMINDER

✦ Mindfulness is paying attention to your present moment experience, on purpose, with curiosity and kindness to yourself. It's about being aware of what you're doing while you're doing it, with a non-judgmental attitude.

✦ There are many different ways to practise mindfulness. One way is to learn mindfulness meditation. Another way is to use daily mindfulness practices where you pause, breathe and bring moment-to-moment awareness to an aspect of your everyday life, for example, the brushing of your teeth.

✦ There are three common forms of mindfulness meditation: focused attention, open monitoring and loving kindness (compassion).

✦ To practise mindfulness meditation, all you need is your body and your breath.

✦ Consider your intention and motivation before you start to meditate and remember that you can practise anywhere, in any position.

✦ It's normal for the mind to wander when you meditate.

✦ There are no strict rules about how often you should meditate, although research shows that the more you practise, the more profound and lasting the benefits will be.

CHAPTER 2

AM I DOING IT RIGHT?

INITIAL CHALLENGES

Many people stop meditating within the first few weeks as they struggle to know whether they're 'doing it right'. In this chapter you'll learn how to overcome some of the difficulties you might encounter when you start to meditate and how to build your daily practice.

Even after making a conscious decision to learn to meditate, it's easy to get distracted. You might persuade yourself that you'll come to it later in the day, or that you'll meditate once you've prepared a snack, answered an email or made a few phone calls. You might find that there's something else that demands your immediate attention. Undoubtedly, building your mindfulness practice requires an element of discipline, as with any new habit. At the outset, it's worth exploring some of the challenges you can expect to face in the first few weeks and months and how to overcome them.

I DON'T HAVE ENOUGH TIME

One of the most common barriers is the feeling that you simply don't have the time to meditate. The irony is however, that practising mindfulness meditation can help you to become more focused, less willing to be distracted and more time efficient. If you can take just a few minutes to still your body and sit quietly on a regular basis, you will soon be able to tap into a sense of calm whenever you need it most. This might be when you're cramped on a commuter train with a child on your knee, when you're dealing with unrealistic deadlines or having to tackle a difficult conversation. I have practised mindfulness in locations as diverse as corridors, cars, courtrooms, trains, toilets and traffic jams. I have practised in meetings, at mealtimes, during family gatherings, at law conferences and even when trying to get my daughter to clean her teeth or get into bed. Without mindfulness, my ability to emerge unscathed would have been seriously

'If you are pressed for time, being in the moment gives you more time by giving you back the fullness of each moment that you have.'

Dr Jon Kabat-Zinn

compromised. Being able to ground myself quickly has marked a real shift in terms of how I tackle stress and interact with my family and friends. My experience has been that mindfulness helps you to repair situations once they've gone wrong by taking criticism less personally and by striving to better understand your adversary, mother, father, friend or child. You become more willing to step forward, offer the olive branch and try again to find a way to get along. Arguments can be averted, voice volume controlled, tone amended and communications restored, to some extent at least.

In terms of benefits in the workplace, finding time for moments of stillness improves your ability to prioritise tasks more efficiently and allows you to gain greater clarity of thought, strengthening your ability to focus and concentrate. Taking a few minutes every day to practise mindfulness meditation can help to extend time by giving you back more of each moment.

I CAN'T SIT STILL TO MEDITATE

It's quite normal to feel unable to sit still when you meditate, even if you're practising for just a few minutes. You might experience discomfort, perhaps a

Tip

Try setting a reminder to prompt you to take a few minutes every day to meditate. Use a Post-it note, an alarm on your phone, or a sticker on the bathroom mirror.

sense of boredom or even start thinking about how you could be spending your time 'more productively'.

If such thoughts or feelings arise, rather than criticising yourself, see if you can notice how your body reacts to being asked to be still. Label what you discover, such as 'a burning desire to scratch my leg', 'an aching lower back', 'a sense of irritation about being here right now when I should be writing a report'. Once labelled, notice if the thoughts and sensations fade away of their own accord or whether you need to adjust your posture, or take a moment to scratch. Do what you need to in order to be able to carry on, with kindness to yourself.

MEDITATION SOUNDS BORING

When my daughter was younger, I remember relishing the opportunity to take just a few minutes for myself to refill my tank. Aside from the joys that parenting can bring, it can also be an exhausting, lonely and often thankless task. There might even come a point when you wonder whether all the vigour you once had will ever return, or whether your old self has gone for ever. In the early years, taking five minutes to meditate enabled me to return to any scenes of chaos, refusals to eat food or unreasonable demands with a sense of healthy distance and renewed energy. Valuable moments of meditation helped me to connect, be present and enjoy the uniqueness of parenting my daughter. So if you're struck by a sense of boredom, see if you can adjust your mindset and view the practice as a slice of valuable, guilt-free time out for yourself.

'Your goal is not to battle with the mind, but to witness the mind.'

Swami Muktananda

MY MIND ZIPS AROUND WHEN I MEDITATE

When you start to meditate, you may feel unable to calm or slow the speed at which your thoughts arise. You might even notice your thoughts zipping from one to the other. If this is your experience, which is very common, simply notice it and witness your mind running fast. It's estimated that the average person has approximately

60–70,000 thoughts per day.[5] It's not surprising then that you may feel that there's little respite from the thinking, doing mind. Be reassured that as your practice develops, the speed at which your thoughts arise tends to slow down, but each experience will be different, so see if you can bring an attitude of acceptance and curiosity to how it is to meditate.

'In mindfulness meditation, you don't try to push thoughts away or wall yourself off from them. Instead, the aim is to be aware of whatever is happening moment by moment, including your thoughts, with a non-reactive attitude.'

Vidyamala Burch

ISN'T MEDITATION COMPLICATED AND LONG-WINDED?

A common misconception about mindfulness meditation is that it's complicated and long-winded – in fact, it's neither. Even thirty seconds of practice can make a difference to your ability to respond in the most stressful of situations. Taking a mindful pause of just three deep breaths before entering a meeting, delivering a speech or sending an email is capable of changing the course of your day.

SIMPLE TIPS TO BUILD YOUR PRACTICE

When you start meditating, and in fact, at any point thereafter, you may experience a scattered mind or feel unable to settle for very long. In order to build your practice, it's useful to aim to meditate for just a few minutes each day, at times that make sense for you. Bolster your formal meditation time with some daily mindfulness practices.

In order to keep going, you'll need to be able to incorporate mindfulness into your daily routine, which is one of the most difficult challenges. Find what works for you, start small and keep going. If you stop, forget, or lose your way, you can always begin again. There's no need to jump to the conclusion that it's not for you, or that you can't even meditate!

You can increase the length of time you practise as you feel able to sit for longer. Most of all, be gentle with yourself and remember that you don't have to like it in order to reap the benefits. So meditate even when you don't want to, and see what happens.

Research shows that meditative benefits are cumulative and emerge over time. Whatever you do, try not to criticise yourself for not meditating.

Instead, consider ways to get yourself back on track. This may involve finding a local group to join, reading an article on the subject, or subscribing to a magazine on mindfulness to help support your practice. Consider whether it's something you can share with friends, family or colleagues and whether this might provide some form of support. You might discover, as I did, that once you talk about your mindfulness with others, there are like-minded people in your community who are keen to share resources, websites, retreats and ideas. Above all, remain open, curious and inquisitive towards the development of your practice and any benefits you start to feel.

> '*When you start learning to meditate, it takes a loooong time to learn this simple lesson: Stop trying so hard.*'
>
> *Barry Boyce*

DAILY MINDFULNESS

In this chapter, the daily practices invite you to set a positive intention for the day ahead, breathe deeply at your desk, bring mindfulness into your morning routine and follow a simple recipe at home.

WORKPLACE

Setting a Positive Intention

Before you begin your work for the day, try setting a positive intention. It may be for example, 'I will listen fully to my fellow colleagues', 'I intend to remain open and receptive to new opportunities' or 'I intend to stay calm and focused'. Write your intention down, keep it simple and reflect on it at the end of the day. Consider what impact, if any, it has on your decision-making and attitude at work.

WORKPLACE

The One-minute Desk Practice

I use the following practice at work, before and often during meetings, or when I have to engage in difficult conversations. Knowing that I can tap into my breath at any time to help restore a sense of stability has saved me on countless occasions from making bad decisions and snappy errors of judgment.

The Practice: If it helps, set a one-minute timer before you begin, then close your eyes or lower your gaze and slowly breathe in and out, focusing on your breath. Feel your points of contact with the ground and rest your hands on the desk or on your lap. Follow the sensation of just one breath – and then another, for one minute. Notice the slight pause at the end of each in-breath and out-breath. Sense the temperature of your breath as it flows in and out of your nostrils and the rise and fall of your chest. When the mind wanders into thinking, worrying or planning, simply bring it back to the breath, as your point of anchor to the present moment. Resume your activities and see if you can bring a sense of calm with you into the rest of your day.

HOME

The Morning Routine

Most of us dash through the morning routine in an effort to get through the door. Whether it's trains to catch or children to drop, somehow mornings can be a source of stress, tinged with a sense of 'Groundhog Day'. It's often a struggle to emerge with any positive intention intact. This week, see if it is possible to use an aspect of your morning routine to bring mindfulness into the start of your day.

The Practice: Run your morning bath or shower and feel the temperature, pressure and texture of the water. Listen to the sound it makes. Notice how it feels. When your mind wanders, return it gently to the physical sensation of the water, for just a few more minutes. How does this experience differ from your normal routine and how does it make you feel?

HOME

A Mindful Recipe

A daily activity that can guide you naturally into a state of mindfulness is cooking. Friends of mine describe late-night baking after the children have gone to bed or the preparation of a simple meal after work as 'time out' from the busyness of the day. If you like to cook, and don't view it as a chore, see if you can take advantage of this time and choose something you love to make – whether it's pancakes, bread, quiche, curry or a simple salad.

Take your time to consider the ingredients, their source, scent, texture and weight. Immerse yourself in the preparation process by focusing entirely on the food. When your mind wanders, gently bring it back to the process and breathe deeply. Relish the time you have taken for yourself to be with the food, rather than cooking simply as a means to an end.

Sometimes mindful moments arise spontaneously. On the first day of spring sunshine, I sat with my daughter on the doorstep eating home-made spiced buns. It was a few minutes of simply 'being' – tasting the food and soaking up the warmth of the sun. Look out for these precious, unexpected times. There are more opportunities for mindfulness than you think.

'When you are mindful of this moment, you are present for your life and your experience just as it is ... not as you hoped it would be ... but for exactly what is here as it unfolds.'

Janice Marturano

* MINDFULNESS MEDITATION *

The Three-minute Breathing Space

This meditation focuses on the movement of your breath. In order to stay alert, it's useful to practise in a seated position, making sure your back is straight. Take a moment to shrug your shoulders and release any tension from your jaw. Focus on stilling the body and returning your wandering mind to the movement of your breath. Listen to the three-minute breathing space meditation.

A QUICK REMINDER

+ If you feel as though you don't have time to meditate, remember that with practice, it can help you to be more focused and time efficient. If you can take just a few minutes to still your body and sit quietly on a regular basis, you will soon be able to find a sense of calm, whenever you need it most.

+ When you meditate, if you feel the need to move, adjust, shift, itch or release, tune in to the feelings and sensations that arise. With kindness to yourself, do what you need to in order to carry on.

+ If you're struck by a sense of boredom when you meditate, see if you can view the practice as valuable guilt-free time out for yourself.

+ If your mind starts to jump from one thought to the next, simply notice your experience. Allow the mind to run fast and with time, the speed at which your thoughts arise will begin to slow down. Taking just three deep breaths can make a difference to your ability to respond in stressful situations.

+ Mindfulness meditation is neither complicated nor long-winded. Reflect on what motivates you to want to carry on and how you're going to remember to do it on a daily basis.

+ Consider finding a local group to join, reading an article on the subject or subscribing to a magazine on mindfulness to support your practice.

CHAPTER 3

IT'S GOOD FOR YOU

When you start to meditate, you may want to be able to assess the benefits and rate its ability to make a difference. Although our desire to 'weigh and measure' is normal, most of the benefits of mindfulness are individually felt. I have found that over time, my ability to focus and pay attention has improved, I have a stronger sense of empathy towards others, and a better understanding of when I'm at risk of being emotionally hijacked. I feel less frazzled at the end of a day, more willing to take risks, and better able to seize new opportunities that I might have previously declined.

'Note that an individual thought does not last long. It is impermanent. If it comes, it will go. Be aware of this.'

Dr Jon Kabat-Zinn

If you can take a few mindful breaths to help navigate life's challenges, you may find yourself able to respond more calmly when your teenager storms off, your colleague is rude, you're lost for words or you simply feel like giving up. This chapter explores why mindfulness meditation is good for you, how it can reduce your stress, increase your ability to focus and help tame your inner critical voice. There are some answers to frequently asked questions, daily mindfulness practices and a uniqueness of breath meditation.

HOW IS IT GOING TO HELP?

I am frequently asked, 'How is mindfulness meditation going to make a difference?' and 'What are the likely benefits?' People often want to know the answers before they begin and even engage in a cost-benefit analysis to ensure a solid return on their investment. It may be reassuring to know that there are now over 4,500 peer-reviewed research papers on the mental, physical and emotional benefits of mindfulness.

Research shows that regular mindfulness meditation practice improves your concentration, ability to pay attention, decision-making and working memory. It reduces stress, lowers your heart rate and blood pressure, strengthens the immune system, and reduces anxiety and depression. It even reduces hyperactivity in ADHD sufferers and alleviates insomnia.[6] Mindfulness encourages emotional stability by enabling you to observe your feelings rather than getting caught up in the drama of how you perceive life to be. It boosts self-esteem and teaches you to appreciate daily life as it unfolds, in all its majesty and travesty.

CASE STUDY: DEPRESSION AND ANXIETY

A study in 2016 in the US followed twenty-nine patients who suffered from depression and anxiety. On average they took part in four sixty-minute acceptance and mindfulness-based group sessions.

The results showed that their symptoms of depression and anxiety decreased significantly over the course of the four visits.[7]

Those with a regular practice report increased feelings of happiness, peace of mind and improved listening skills. Another significant benefit is the ability of mindfulness to create mental space to enable you to *respond*, rather than *react* instinctively, or out of habit. Being able to expand the space and time you have to *reflect* before you decide how to *act*, can mean the difference between triggering a bitter row and enabling a moment of frustration to pass almost unnoticed.

STRESS

In everyday language, stress is a feeling that people have when they are overloaded and struggling to cope with too many demands. There's a difference between feeling under pressure, which is often accompanied by an element of control, and feeling stressed out. While stress helps the body prepare in the face of danger and is essential to survival, chronic stress can undermine a person's mental and physical health. People experience stress in different ways. It may manifest itself as fatigue, feelings of anxiety, headaches, a loss of temper or even depression. In the workplace it's becoming increasingly necessary to find effective antidotes to deal with excessive workloads, long working days, increasing responsibilities and short deadlines.

Within my own profession, the first well-being survey conducted in 2015 at the Bar, showed that one in three barristers found it difficult to control or stop worrying. Two in three individuals felt that showing signs of stress was a sign of weakness, while one in six reported feeling in low spirits most of the time.[8] Fifty-nine per cent of those surveyed stated that unhealthy levels of perfectionism and the notion of well-being were rarely spoken about at the Bar. In the 2018 'Resilience and Well-being Survey' report by the Junior Lawyers Division of the Law Society of England and Wales, over eighty-two per cent of solicitors reported either regularly or occasionally feeling stressed, with twenty-six per cent of those feeling severely or extremely stressed.[9]

Similar statistics have emerged in the US. Out of nearly 13,000 employed attorneys, twenty-eight per cent reported that they were suffering from depression, nineteen per cent with anxiety and twenty-three per cent with stress.[10] Worryingly, nearly twenty-one per cent reported that they were struggling with 'problematic drinking'. In 2016, The National Task Force on Lawyer Well-Being in the US reported that the current state of lawyers' health could not support a 'profession dedicated to client service and dependent on public trust'.[11] Perhaps this is merely the tip of the professional iceberg, as other industries have reported similar worrying statistics.[12] In the UK, work-stress-related illness now accounts for half of all working days lost due to ill-health.

So what happens to your body and your brain when you get stressed? Research in this area is growing rapidly and the findings are fascinating. Neuroscientists now know that there are two pathways in the brain that trigger the stress response. The first pathway is where you encounter something in your environment which makes you react physically (for example, the sight of a snake). The second pathway involves thoughts (for example, worries about public speaking at work next week).

The first pathway involves a part of your brain called the **thalamus**, which sends visual information directly to the **amygdala** (an almond-shaped structure known as the fear centre). The **amygdala** then sends a distress signal to another part of your brain, called the **hypothalamus**. This acts as a command and control centre communicating with your **autonomic nervous system**, which has two parts – the **sympathetic** and the **parasympathetic**. It's the sympathetic nervous system which triggers what is known as the fight-flight-freeze stress response. This leads to the release of **adrenaline and other hormones** into the bloodstream, which enables your heart to beat faster and increases your pulse rate and blood flow to your muscles. Breathing becomes more rapid, your senses sharpen and **cortisol** is released, which enables the body to remain on high alert.

The second pathway involves worried or anxious thoughts in the brain's **prefrontal cortex** (which is involved in decision-making) that can trigger the **amygdala,** which then kick-starts the stress response. The **prefrontal cortex** can also keep the **amygdala** in check when it overreacts by dampening down the stress response if it decides, for instance, that what sounded like gunfire was actually the sound of a car backfiring.

In a stress-prone brain, the amygdala will be quick to react to what it perceives as a threat and the prefrontal cortex (battling with anxious thoughts) will often be unable to 'reason' away or stop the stress response. Neuroscientists have noted that 'the amygdala of a person trained in mindfulness is less likely to respond to a neutral situation like public speaking as threatening, perhaps because his or her amygdala is actually smaller and less reactive'.[13] Meanwhile, the cortex of the more mindful brain has weaker connections to the amygdala, which makes it less likely to be triggered in the first place.

Staying in stress mode for any length of time can damage the body's blood vessels and arteries, which can in turn increase blood pressure and raise the risk of heart attacks and strokes. Prolonged bouts of stressful thoughts and feelings weaken your immune system and lead to anxiety and depression. While the heightened state of alert of the stress mode once helped to protect us from the physical threat of the sabre-toothed tiger, in today's world the same ancient biological reactions are as easily triggered by contemporary worries, such as forgetting to hit save on a draft document or losing your mobile phone.

Mindfulness meditation is a proven way of activating your **parasympathetic nervous system**, or **'rest and digest' system** as it's more commonly known. This reduces the harmful levels of stress hormones released into the body when the fight-flight-freeze response is activated. Engaging this part of the nervous system is a reliable way of regulating the impact of stress.

When strong feelings arise, mindfulness allows you to recognise their arrival and stops you from being dragged down the street by their strength or persistence. It brings you out of stress mode and creates *mind-space*, which allows you to appraise a situation more dispassionately, so you can decide how best to respond.

People with a regular mindfulness practice often report feeling less stressed and more emotionally balanced. One of the reasons for this is that as you continue to meditate, your brain changes physically, a process known as **neuroplasticity**. This concept refers to the lifelong capacity of the brain to change and rewire itself in response to the stimulation of learning and experience. Scientific research in the field of mindfulness meditation shows that a regular practice leads to the cerebral cortex (the outer layer of the brain) becoming thicker in three key areas. These are the prefrontal cortex – the part that controls attention – the insula – the

'Structurally, the brain is in a class of its own, with over one hundred billion processing units (neurons) – on the order of stars in the core of the Milky Way galaxy.'

Gazzaley and Rosen

part used for tuning into others and ourselves – and the hippocampus – the part that regulates your visual and spatial memory. These changes help to explain how meditation improves your ability to pay attention, gain greater self-awareness and experience more empathy towards others. Regular meditation also helps to reduce the reactivity of the amygdala – the part of the brain responsible for memory of emotions, especially fear – and the triggering of the fight-flight-freeze stress response. Evidence suggests that such brain changes start to emerge with long-term meditation practice. Results are inconclusive at present as to the extent to which change can be expected from a short-term practice of weeks or months.

CASE STUDY: THE YOUNG BRAIN

A study at UCLA in the US found that meditation slows the usual shrinkage of the brain as people get older. It showed that at fifty years of age, long-term meditators' brains are younger by seven and a half years compared to the brains of non-meditators of the same age.[14]

So the next time you're feeling stressed, see if you can notice the physical symptoms that arise – perhaps a clenched jaw, stiff shoulders, a nervous stomach or an overall feeling of tension in the body. Take a moment to pause and breathe deeply, unclench, loosen, release and let go. Rest in your breath and pause to be present, knowing that you can activate your parasympathetic nervous system's natural ability to switch off the stress response at any time of the day or night. Once you're able to detect the physical onset of stress, it becomes much easier to mitigate its effect. Taking a moment to notice and breathe can help to release the build up of tension throughout the day.

FOCUS AND ATTENTION

Distractions are on the rise. People are now connected to their screens and smartphones for significant amounts of the day and night, often multitasking between them. The lure of social media, the expectation of an instant response to emails and the constant demand for high productivity mean that our ability to pay attention, and focus on the task in hand is under threat.

Interference comes in two forms – as distractions arising from irrelevant information and as interruptions.[15] Both are capable of derailing us from accomplishing our tasks.

In terms of distractions, research in the US shows that adults and teenagers now check their phones up to one hundred and fifty times a day.[16] Similar studies in the UK show that people check their smartphones, on average every twelve minutes of the day. Forty per cent of us look at our phone within five minutes of waking up, climbing to sixty-five per cent of those aged under thirty-five.[17] The art of getting someone's undivided attention in the workplace or at home is under sustained attack. Even the simple pleasures of eating together, watching a family film, or going for a walk have been affected by the invasive habit of phone checking, texting and Internet surfing. Holidays have also been impacted with eight in ten smartphone users taking their devices away with them to check in on what's going on back home.[18]

'Attention determines our degree of intimacy with our ordinary experiences and contours our entire sense of connection to life.'

Sharon Salzberg

In the workplace, interference has now become the norm. For many, traditional working hours have been supplanted by a 24/7 experience of connectivity. There's an expectation that instant messages will be answered and emails responded to, within record time, even if it means taking your focused attention away from something more substantial.

At home, a smartphone is often found at the dinner table, in the bedroom and even the bathroom. In recent years there has been a significant rise in FOMO (the fear of missing out) and in Nomophobia (the fear of being out of mobile phone contact). It's not only teenagers who are struggling to manage the expectations and demands of constant connectivity. It's also their parents, who may be physically present, but mentally elsewhere, monitoring information, flitting between mail accounts or updating their social media.

'What information consumes is rather obvious: it consumes the attention of its recipients. Hence a wealth of information creates a poverty of attention, and a need to allocate that attention efficiently among the overabundance of information sources that might consume it.'

Herbert Simon

These forms of interference contribute to the common experience of feeling distracted and impact significantly on our ability to pay attention and work efficiently. One study of managers and employees in the US found that those who used their smartphones for work at night after nine o'clock in the evening showed impaired cognitive control at work the following day, and suffered from a reduced ability to pay attention.[19]

CASE STUDY: DISTRACTION

One study in the UK found that after dealing with an email, which itself took an average of just under two minutes, it took the workers an average of sixty-eight seconds – more than half of the time required to read and respond to that email – to return to their work and remember what they were doing. [20]

Our desire to stay connected to the lives of others, and to check-in constantly with what's going on elsewhere, means that we risk missing valuable moments in our own lives. We become distracted, get less done, withdraw more and feel dissatisfied when our experience doesn't live up to the world of others portrayed on social media. Gone are the days when friends would call long distance for a catch-up and hatch plans for the future. Diaries are full, lives are packed and kids are constantly on the go, with weekends often arranged months ahead. But this frenetic style of 'doing', coupled with the demands of our online lives, is often at the cost of connection with people in the 'real' world.

'Everyone knows what attention is. It is the taking possession by the mind, in clear and vivid form, of one out of what seem several simultaneously possible objects or trains of thought.'

William James

So how can mindfulness meditation improve our ability to pay attention and appreciate the life we have? It's clear that the practice helps us to notice what's going on right now and to let go of any thoughts or feelings that distract us from our present moment experience. But it goes much further than that, as mindfulness meditation gives us a *perspective* on what's going on around us and *strengthens* our ability to be present. As a consequence, we become less willing to be distracted when focusing on a task that requires completion. Over time, these abilities become naturally ingrained in our way of being and impact the way we respond to situations, friends and colleagues, as we choose how to spend our valuable time.

Mindfulness also helps us to develop an attitude of non-judgmental acceptance of how things are, however difficult or uncomfortable this may be. This attitude differs from our normal tendency to judge experiences as good or bad. If we're able to let go of making judgments, and see things as they really are, this helps to bring both clarity and relief from the constant pressure for life to be different, better, or even elsewhere.

Tip:

Use mindfulness to see beneath a rough exterior. When someone acts unpleasantly or is simply difficult, it's often hard to feel any compassion for them. More often than not you feel resentful or angry. However, if you can pause and recognise your own feelings, you can soften and create an opening for the possibility of greater connection with those around you.

A recent comprehensive review of mindfulness research concluded that the average meditator had stronger attention skills than seventy-two per cent of non-meditators.[21] When you consider the practice of mindfulness meditation, this all makes sense given that:

✦ Every time you return to a point of anchor when you meditate, you build your ability to concentrate.

✦ Every time you're kind to yourself when the mind wanders, you exercise and strengthen your ability to be compassionate when challenging moments arise.

✦ Every time you notice where the mind has wandered to, you have an opportunity for insight into its habits and patterns.

CASE STUDY: IMPROVEMENTS TO ATTENTION

One of the most extensive studies on how meditation improves your ability to focus was published in 2018. It offered evidence that intensive and continued meditation is associated with enduring improvements in sustained attention.

The experiment began in 2011 when the authors assessed participants, who ranged from twenty-two to sixty-nine years old, before and after they attended a three-month retreat at the Shambhala Mountain Center in Colorado. The participants underwent various types of meditation training, such as sustaining focus on objects, practising mindful breathing techniques and generating positive feelings of compassion and loving kindness for others and themselves. The immediate findings from the study, published after the retreat, revealed that the training enhanced the participants' emotional well-being and enabled them to perform better on tasks related to focus. Seven years later, when researchers checked back in with the group, all of the participants reported that they continued to meditate in some capacity. It was found that the more they meditated, the better they maintained the benefits of their training seven years earlier. This was especially true for the older participants.[22]

INNER CRITICAL VOICE

Negative thoughts such as 'I'm not clever enough', 'I'm a failure', or 'I'm useless' can appear almost audibly like a soundtrack in the mind. They belong to the inner critical voice which is a type of dialogue that pops in and out of our conscious thinking and takes the form of ideas, suggestions, thoughts and expressions that guide behaviour. In essence, the inner critical voice is the familiar negative tune our mind starts to hum to remind us of how useless or inadequate it deems us to be. Over time, it can diminish self-esteem and impact negatively on our ability to make decisions.

It's the voice of disgust and disappointment. It's the harsh, judgmental way we speak to ourselves in a tone we would never use with a friend. It's also very keen on the words 'should have' and 'would have'. Sometimes, the inner critical voice is so powerful that it can feel like a core part of our identity. Some people view it as a necessary evil to drive them on to

'Our thoughts are like rumours in the mind. They might be true, but then again, they might not be.'

Mark Williams and Danny Penman

achieve better results, but in reality, it serves only to reinforce a sense of unworthiness.

'Try giving your inner critic a persona, with a name and a wardrobe. Offer them a nice cup of tea and a nap. They must be exhausted from constantly going over all those negative thoughts.'

Sharon Salzberg

In the workplace, our inner critical voice might try to convince us that we're not popular or that we will never attain the professional heights we seek. It might persuade us that 'life is elsewhere' and that we're not good enough to get what we think we want, in order to feel satisfied.

The first step towards taming the inner critical voice is to notice its arrival. This is easier said than done as we're so used to hearing it that it can feel as though it's intimately connected to who we are. This is where the practice of mindfulness comes in useful, as it helps us to notice when the inner critical voice starts to speak.

The next time it appears, see if you can hear what it says, notice how often it visits and how it makes you feel. You might want to label it in some way, such as, 'negative voice telling me I'm not quick enough' or 'self-defeating voice of doom before I've even started'. In response, choose to acknowledge its presence and gently invite it to leave, for example, by quietly saying to yourself something like: 'Oh, there you are again, telling me I'm not good enough … I'm not listening …time to move on.' Ultimately, the inner critical voice is often a symptom of stress or exhaustion. Noticing how vicious your own commentary can be often provides a much-needed moment for reflection. See if you can replace or soften its content with self-compassionate words of kindness, such as 'I'm strong enough' or 'capable enough' to carry on. Ultimately, by befriending the mind and understanding its habits, you become less vulnerable to the impact of negative thoughts when they do arise and less prone to being trampled by the demands of your own perfectionism.

FREQUENTLY ASKED QUESTIONS

WHAT HAPPENS IF I FALL ASLEEP?

When I started meditating, I remember falling asleep regularly during the body scan mediation that formed part of an eight-week mindfulness programme. The teacher would lead us through the meditation and without fail I would miss at least half of it, sleeping through until I heard the sound of the bell which drew the practice to a close. I always remember the teacher's kindness and reassuring words as the six of us staggered back into a seated position – with no mention of our heavy breathing or intermittent snoring. She gently reminded us that while we were no longer meditating at that point, the experience was useful in its own right as it was a good indicator that we needed more sleep.

To avoid falling asleep, it helps to practise in a seated position, as it's less conducive to drifting off. With meditation, one of the aims is to gently fall awake to the present moment, just as it is. But rest reassured, that if you do fall asleep, you're not alone.

WHEN I MEDITATE, SHOULD I BREATHE IN ANY PARTICULAR WAY?

There is no requirement to breathe in any particular way when you meditate. Simply allow your breath to be natural and observe its rise and fall.

WHAT DO I DO WITH INCOMING THOUGHTS?

During a meditation, when incoming thoughts arise, as they will, simply notice them, and label them if it helps, for example *planning, imagining, judging*. Then allow them to pass and see how quickly they disappear, if you let them. By practising in this way, you gently start to separate your attachment to your thoughts, which means that you're less likely to be overwhelmed by them.

HOW WILL I FEEL WHEN I MEDITATE?

Everyone responds differently to mindfulness meditation. The experience is unique and changes on a daily basis. Some people feel a sense of relaxation, either during or after a session, and increased energy levels. Others experience feelings of irritation or restlessness, especially when starting out.

I remember leading a meditation with a group of beginners, which involved asking them to visualise a lake. One of the students explained to me at the end that she struggled to imagine her lake, as in spite of my guidance, she was wracked with indecision as to which lake to choose. She even felt dissatisfied with her eventual choice and frustrated that she felt so distracted. While these feelings were uncomfortable, she explained to me that for her they were nonetheless useful in revealing her current state of mind.

Bringing an attitude of friendliness and curiosity to your experience can make all the difference. So take a moment to reflect on how the bringing of a compassionate mind-set might positively impact the way you feel about your practice. Use the journal at the back of the book to note down what resonates with you and why.

IS MINDFULNESS RELIGIOUS?

The simple answer is no. Based originally on the historical teachings of the Buddha, it was the seminal work of Dr Jon Kabat-Zinn in the late 1970s that brought mindfulness to the masses as a secular practice. Mindfulness is often described as a form of mental training and is a basic human capability that anyone can learn.

DAILY MINDFULNESS

In this chapter, the daily mindfulness practices focus on how to bring a mindful attitude towards managing your inbox and navigating meetings. There's also a mindful eating and walking practice.

WORKPLACE

Email and Internet

Reading and replying to emails often distracts us from completing our work during the day. They ping into the inbox or indiscriminately slide across the screen. The completion of the small tasks they demand releases dopamine (the pleasure hormone) in the brain. This in turn fuels our desire to read emails as they arrive, which compromises our ability to pay attention to other aspects of work.

Overleaf are a few ideas to consider in order to bring a more mindful approach to your email communications and Internet usage.

✦ Keep your smartphone, laptop and any other such device out of the bedroom and see if you can avoid checking your emails first thing in the morning when you wake up.

✦ Consider silencing your smartphone at certain times of the day.

✦ Remove your smartphone from your vision when working on substantive tasks. Research shows that the mere presence of a phone on your desk can lead to distraction and reduced levels of performance.[23]

✦ Consider setting up an email notification informing people as to when you will be checking your emails.

✦ See if you can refrain from checking your emails before or after working hours and during the weekend. Many companies are now adopting policies that place clear limits on sending emails after hours.

✦ Consider switching off notifications on all devices, for certain parts of the day.

✦ If you need to use the Internet at work, try using only one screen at a time. Simply minimising numerous screens can be too much of a temptation for the brain to re-engage with the Internet before you have completed the task in hand.

✦ If you find yourself flitting between emails, the Internet, social media and substantive tasks, see if you can at least be mindful of the fact that you're doing so. Then consider whether you wish to continue, and if so, for how long, or whether you want to return to your work. A seemingly brief interruption can lead to a disproportionate loss of time.

✦ Refrain from using screens for at least an hour before you go to bed. The blue light emitted by screens on mobile phones, computers, tablets and televisions, inhibits the production of melatonin, the hormone that controls your sleep/wake cycle. Reducing melatonin makes it harder to fall and stay asleep.

Rather than a complete digital detox, which is often no more effective than a crash diet, try introducing a few new sustainable boundaries to support your mindfulness practice which allow you to focus more fully on those tasks that require your undivided attention.

WORKPLACE

Meetings

As you walk to your next meeting venue, take a few deep breaths and slow your pace. Take your time to arrive.

The Practice: Once in the meeting room, see how it feels to stay silent for the first few moments, letting everyone arrive physically and mentally. Take in your surroundings and notice how you're sitting. Relax your shoulders and perhaps adopt the hint of a smile. Notice your body language and that of others. See if you can truly listen and consider how you engage. Return to following your natural breath at intervals during the meeting. Notice how you feel.

Consider: How does this experience differ from your usual meetings at work? Consider whether you could incorporate some white space (free time) between back-to-back meetings to allow time to arrive, reflect and participate more meaningfully. For me, these simple techniques have significantly changed the dynamics of many meetings – for the better.

HOME

Mindful Eating

Mindful eating is a form of food meditation. Research shows that eating mindfully improves digestion, regulates appetite and helps you to notice and enjoy the taste of your food.

How often do you eat without truly being aware of what you're eating? Are you a speedy eater or do you take your time to really savour your food? This week try to incorporate some moments of mindful eating.

Choose a particular meal or a snack and eat with mindful awareness that you're eating. Chew slowly and focus your attention on the smell, taste, texture and origin of the food. You may choose to eat in silence or share the experience with others. It can be quite fun!

Here are a few suggestions to get you started:

✦ Take time to prepare the food. Notice any feelings or thoughts that arise without trying to change them.

✦ When eating mindfully, simply eat. Ensure there are no devices at the table.

✦ If a mindful meal is not realistic, choose a piece of fruit or something nutritious that you can eat mindfully during a break.

✦ Slow down and stop eating when you're full. The body sends a signal that it's had enough food about twenty minutes after the brain, which is why we often overeat.

✦ Once you've finished eating, become aware of your body and tune in to your breath. Notice any feelings of fullness or tastes that linger.

HOME

Mindful Walking

With mindful walking, you drop into your senses and your body. The Zen Buddhist teacher Thich Nhat Hanh explains that: 'In our daily lives, we may spend many hours forgetting the body. We get lost in our computer or in our worries, fear or busyness…Walking meditation unites our body and our mind".[24]

The Practice: You can use this practice anywhere – between the floors of a building, as you walk to your car or stroll through the park.

Mindful walking can be practised in different ways – in slow motion or at natural walking speed. In this practice, try walking slowly, but not so much so that you draw attention to yourself. Experience what you see, feel and hear around you. Open your senses. Feel the ground beneath you and the shifting weight of your body. Notice the way you walk and how you place your feet. When your mind wanders, come back time and time again to the physical sensation of walking. Notice the movement of your body with each step. Think about how you can incorporate a mindful walk into your daily routine.

* MINDFULNESS MEDITATION *

Uniqueness of Breath Meditation

For this focused-attention meditation, you can either adopt a seated position or lie down. If you're lying down, make sure your legs are uncrossed and your shoulders are relaxed. See if you can maintain a sense of alertness to reduce the chance of falling asleep. You can either close your eyes or lower your gaze — whichever is more comfortable for you.

This meditation invites you to become aware of the uniqueness of each breath. Notice any sensations or thoughts that arise, and return to the breath as your anchor to the present moment. Bring the mind back to this point of focus every time it wanders. Do this with kindness to yourself. Listen to the uniqueness of breath meditation.

A QUICK REMINDER

✦ Mindfulness meditation is good for you. It improves concentration, increases your ability to pay attention and make decisions. It creates mental space in which you can choose to respond rather than react to life's challenges. It also helps to strengthen the immune system and reduce insomnia, anxiety and depression.

✦ Mindfulness meditation is a proven way of activating your parasympathetic nervous system (rest and digest system) and reducing harmful levels of stress hormones, which flood your body when the fight-flight-freeze response is activated.

✦ As you continue to meditate, your brain changes physically, a process known as neuroplasticity. Scientific research shows that a regular practice of mindfulness meditation leads to the cerebral cortex (the outer layer of the brain) becoming thicker in three key areas – the prefrontal cortex, the insula and the hippocampus.

✦ Mindfulness meditation helps to tame your inner critical voice by enabling you to become aware of its presence and tone.

✦ When you start to practise mindfulness meditation you may fall asleep. Try a seated position to maintain awareness.

✦ Mindfulness is a basic human capability and is not owned by any group, religion or philosophy. It's simple, secular and supported by scientific research.

CHAPTER 4

TOO WORRIED TO SETTLE?

Within less than a second, the mind is capable of racing between thoughts. Before even getting out of bed, you might find yourself worrying about whether you've paid the gas bill, how to deal with a difficult colleague or whether or not to apply for a new job. It's a cacophony of big, small, important and mundane, racing thoughts – and it's exhausting. No wonder it's often hard for the mind to steady itself.

In this chapter, we examine how mindfulness can settle a busy mind and how the practice can help to tackle our worries and anxiety. There are some answers to frequently asked questions, daily mindfulness practices and a body-scan meditation.

SETTLING A BUSY MIND

The best work intentions are often thwarted by a distracted, busy mind. With so many conflicting demands and time constraints, it can be hard to commit to concentrated work even when a quiet moment does arise. It often takes longer than anticipated to complete a task, particularly when your mind is not truly engaged or present.

So what can you do to quiet a busy mind? One way is to settle the body. Take a few moments to scan through your body, checking for any tension. To do this, close your eyes or lower your gaze and focus your mind on one area at a time, as you breathe in and out. You might want to start at your feet and slowly work your way up to the top of your head. Notice what arises as you bring your attention to different areas of your body, becoming aware of any stiffness, aches or pains that you may encounter. Breathe into these areas, without judgment or blame, and simply notice how your body feels at this moment in time. By dropping into your bodily sensations, you bring yourself naturally into the present moment, which has the effect of reducing mental chatter. There is a body-scan meditation at the end of this chapter for you to listen to and notice how you feel.

Another way to settle the mind is to get out into nature. Becoming aware of the enormity of the night sky or the vastness of the ocean reminds us that there is something bigger than ourselves. It gives us a sense of perspective and an understanding that at any point in time, we can shift our attention away from stress-inducing thoughts to the vista in front of us, wherever we may be. Moderate sunlight exposure, even on an overcast day, helps to improve mood and focus by boosting serotonin (a happiness hormone) levels in the body. Sunlight is also known to decrease the risk of depression in those who suffer from seasonal affective disorder (SAD). Even more reason then to leave the building and find a physical space to *be*, rather than *do*.

In addition to the challenge of settling down, many people struggle to get relief from overthinking, ruminating and catastrophising. Rumination is the tendency to rehash the same thoughts, usually negative ones, over and over again. While catastrophic thinking is characterised by a downward spiral of negative thoughts and outcomes, usually triggered by one or two initial worries. A typical catastrophic pattern might look like this:

'I'm going to be late. I'm going to miss my meeting. I knew I should have left earlier. It's my fault. I'm always late. They'll probably sack me – and I won't be able to pay my mortgage – and what's more, I deserve it!'

When you next notice yourself catastrophising or ruminating, see if you can act as a witness to your own mental chatter by consciously bringing your attention to your thoughts without engaging with them. Try saying 'stop', quietly or out loud, before taking several deep breaths. In my classes, whenever I mention rumination or catastrophising, I can almost hear a sigh of relief as people often have a 'Thank goodness, I'm not the only one' moment.

Learning how to quiet a busy mind and reduce the impact of negative or racing thoughts can mean the difference between having a productive day and feeling totally overwhelmed.

WORRY AND ANXIETY

Everyone worries. It's normal. People worry about their jobs, families, the economy, health and these days in particular, the state of the nation. They worry about deadlines, whether their presentation is good enough, how others perceive them and whether they'll be 'found out' as unworthy or simply not good enough.

We worry about being able to pay the mortgage, raise our children, make ends meet and somehow stay sane. Worrying is thought-based and generally involves thinking about the negative outcomes that might take place in the future.

When you start to worry excessively, however, it can significantly affect your well-being and leave you feeling depleted and anxious. With anxiety, it's difficult, if not impossible, to identify its cause or source. The word means a 'condition of agitation or distress' and is often described as a feeling of fear or panic. While small amounts of anxiety can enhance your performance and productivity, moderate to high levels interfere with your ability to function.

> '*When we stop dwelling on the past or worrying about the future, we're open to rich sources of information we've been missing out on – information that can keep us out of the downward spiral and poised for a richer life.*'
>
> Mark Williams

When you feel anxious, you might experience a rapid or irregular heartbeat, sweating, a churning stomach, tense muscles or tight shoulders. You might have trouble sleeping, lack concentration, feel irritable, depressed or lose your self-confidence. Anxiety is often hallmarked by a voice that tells you that 'something's wrong', even when you know rationally that all seems well. It's a feeling with a powerful grip that is capable of stealing your joy before you even get out of bed. In the US, The National Institute of Mental Health (NIMH) estimated that one in five Americans have had some kind of anxiety disorder in the past year. A survey in the UK reported that one in six adults had experienced a 'neurotic health problem' (most commonly anxiety and depression) in the previous week.

A major factor, which contributes to anxiety, is long-term stress. Excessive worrying or anxiety triggers the fight-flight-freeze response, which causes the body's sympathetic nervous system to release stress hormones, such as cortisol. As you saw in chapter 3, practising mindfulness meditation acts as an effective counterbalance to the activation of this response by engaging your 'rest and digest' parasympathetic nervous system. This enables the heart rate to slow, blood pressure to reduce, circulation to improve and digestion to normalise. The good news is that you can't be in two parts of the nervous system at the same time.

Engaging the *rest and digest* system immediately starts to regulate your body and mind.

While you can't stop worrying or cure anxiety altogether, by practising mindfulness, you get better at recognising when they first arise. You become able to stand outside the experience, with slight detachment, so that it becomes merely an experience, rather than something that threatens to overwhelm you. You notice the physical sensations that accompany the feeling, perhaps a knotted stomach, clenched jaw or tension headache. Once you become aware of these sensations, you can choose to breathe consciously for a few moments, engage the parasympathetic nervous system and guide yourself back to a better sense of perspective.

So try using mindfulness the next time you feel anxious about something, whether it's at work, with your children, at home or alone. Notice how focusing on your breathing might help to ground you and bring a sense of steadiness. It's a practice I use whenever I feel worried or angry. If I lose my temper, I still engage mindfulness to avert disaster, as it allows me to repair a situation more quickly, before things get out of hand.

As you have seen in previous chapters, it can be helpful to label your experience, once you notice it, for example 'my stomach's knotted, I feel sick and here comes the worrying thought about how I'm going to pay my tax bill'. With mindfulness, you get to choose to allow the thought to wash over you, rather than let it reign. As Dr Jon Kabat-Zinn says, 'You can't stop the waves, but you can learn to surf'. Engaging the practice in this way prevents a steep descent into despair, a state from which it's often hard to emerge unscathed. While your worries may have substance, there may be little you can do to resolve them by going over and over their all-consuming narrative.

The feeling of anxiety tends to soften if you learn to create a space between yourself and what you're experiencing, by pausing and breathing consciously for a few moments. This *mind space* helps you to acknowledge its presence, rather than pushing it away or denying its existence. In this way, when confronted with difficulty, you might consciously choose to be kind to yourself while recognising that 'this moment is difficult'. You might even ask yourself: 'What is it that I need right now?' as you cultivate a sense of kind responsiveness and self-compassion, instead of habitual, harsh self-judgment.

In essence, mindfulness reminds you that you are in control, not the random thought that has emerged from the side wing, while you weren't looking.

CASE STUDY: REDUCING ANXIETY

In a study in the US led by Dr Jon Kabat-Zinn, researchers from the University of Massachusetts Medical School investigated the effects of a mindfulness-based therapy programme on twenty-two participants with generalised anxiety disorder. Ninety per cent of the participants documented significant reductions in anxiety and depression following an eight-week course.

Those who also suffered from panic attacks had a significant reduction in both attacks and symptoms following the course. At a three-year follow-up, the researchers found that the improvements had been maintained.[25]

FEAR

Many of the stories we tell each other, including the fairy stories we grew up with, revolve around the concept of fear. This universal emotion is caused by the belief that someone or something is dangerous, likely to cause pain, or is a threat in some form. Fear might stem from an ingrained vulnerability or take you completely by surprise. Its aftermath is often devastating and can leave you feeling helpless in its grip.

Fear can halt your progress, prevent you from making a decision, taking a job, leaving a country or repairing a relationship. Fears are concrete, nebulous, real and imagined. They reside in the past, present and future. As a well-known Buddhist teaching explains, 'fear x resistance = suffering'.

In the workplace, it could be the thought of public speaking, presenting a report to your team, sharing your views in meetings or attending an annual staff appraisal that triggers your fear. It may be that you have a fear of missing out (FOMO) on romance, adventure, promotion or fun. Or perhaps you fear you will lose what you love and never quite reach your destination. Of course, it's a necessary emotion that makes you stop, look and listen, when danger is close. The difficulty lies in

'No one ever tells us to stop running away from fear. We are very rarely told to move closer, to just be there, to become familiar with fear... So the next time you encounter fear, consider yourselves lucky. This is where the courage comes in. Usually we think that brave people have no fear. The truth is that they are intimate with fear.'

Pema Chödrön

being able to distinguish between the fear that serves you well and that which prevents you from pursuing your goals. Crucially, fear also triggers the body's fight-flight-freeze stress response.

American psychologist Tara Brach describes what she calls the 'trance of fear', which is where we become trapped and experience life through its filter. It can start to impact our behaviour and restrict our capacity to live life to the full.[26] When we obsess or worry that something is bound to go wrong, our natural human instinct is to try to push the feeling away. Yet Brach explains that when we do this, energetically, it's still there, but it just appears in a different form, for example, as depression, shame or physical illness. By denying the negative emotion, we close ourselves down to 'love, joy and creativity'.[27] Tara Brach explains that meditation provides a strategy to help us recognise this devastating emotion when it hits and to disentangle ourselves from it. With mindfulness, we change the way we relate to this strong emotion, approaching it with openness and curiosity.

By growing your awareness of how fear feels, by labelling what arises ('tight stomach', 'dry mouth', 'shallow breath'), you can breathe, and respond mindfully, rather than reactively or instinctively. You refrain from latching on to the emotion and allowing it to drag you downwards towards an eventual negative outcome, such as doom, despair or debt (it usually starts with a 'd' word for me).

I remember the first time I stood up and delivered a legal argument in an international criminal trial. It was utterly nerve-racking. I had been a lawyer for several years by then and had led my own trials in the UK. But this was different. It was a former president on trial and the time came for me to make my first submissions. I remember feeling nauseous as I tried to focus on my breath. I knew that all I had to do was to get my knees to bend and straighten. Once standing upright directly in front of the judges, the rest would follow naturally. As I rose and locked my knees, I remember the courtroom falling silent. I no longer recall whether I won or lost the point, but the sensation of locking knees, breathing and searching for a steadiness to speak has stayed with me. Today, I know that I can use mindfulness to still my racing thoughts and slow my breathing, which always helps to calm my nerves. It is a powerful, invisible friend.

So while it's not possible or even desirable to eradicate fear, with mindfulness you can modify your response and regain control over the extent to which you are affected by it. You learn to examine your past experiences and hopes for the future in a way that doesn't become obsessive or emotionally damaging as you move outside the 'tangle of fear-thinking'.[28]

NOT ALWAYS EASY...

Mindfulness meditation is simple, but that doesn't mean it's easy. When you start to practise, you want to know whether your experience is as it should be. You want to be reassured that you're at least heading in the right direction – wherever that may be. So here are some more answers to frequently asked questions.

IS IT HELPFUL TO MEDITATE WITH OTHERS?

Meditating with other people can provide an invaluable support network. It gives you an opportunity to share your experience, raise questions and talk through ideas with like-minded people. It also helps to support your motivation to practise privately, just as a weekly piano lesson might encourage you to learn your latest piece. These days, no matter where you live, you should be able to find either a local or online group to join. When I started to meditate, it was the experience of sharing my challenges and vulnerabilities with others that made it somehow more human and possible to carry on. It was great to know that I wasn't the only one who fell asleep or struggled to find time to meditate. It was also a safe space in which to ask the teacher any burning questions I had. This opportunity for group learning helped to sustain and nurture my practice in the first few months, and beyond.

MY BACK ACHES WHEN I MEDITATE – IS THIS NORMAL?

When you sit for any length of time, whether on a cushion on the floor or on a high-backed chair, you may find that your back or shoulders start to ache. Depending on the length of your sitting, if aches arise you might choose to adjust your posture, lean forward or sit further back, to see if this brings relief. Or you might simply notice the ache, breathe into the area and see what happens. On a silent retreat last year, during lengthy meditation sittings, I found that not only did I struggle at times to stay mentally with the practice (as my mind wandered regularly to thoughts about work, lunch, dinner and sleep), but I also struggled physically with lower back pain. Adjusting my posture by leaning forwards and moving gently when I needed to, eased the discomfort. I could then start over by directing my attention back to the breath. Remember that each time you practise, it will be different and while some sittings may be easier 'mentally' than others, you may also find that you are physically challenged and need to shift your position or adjust your posture in order to carry on.

CAN YOU MEDITATE WITH YOUR EYES OPEN?

Yes. If closing your eyes to meditate creates anxiety or fearfulness, meditate with your eyes open, using an unfocused gaze. Visual distractions may come to challenge you, so you'll need to be mindful of this, and return to holding a soft gaze when it happens. One popular practice is to use the flame of a candle as a point of focus. When the mind starts to wander, simply guide it back to the ever-changing appearance of the flame.

DAILY MINDFULNESS

The daily mindfulness practices in this chapter focus on how mindfulness can help you to make better decisions and deal more compassionately with difficult colleagues at work. There's also encouragement to be curious and to see how it feels when you slow down, engage and communicate more mindfully.

WORKPLACE

Improving Decision-making

We make thousands of decisions every day, often without even realising it. Many of us are affected by what is known as 'decision fatigue'. This is where the quality of decision-making deteriorates after a prolonged period. Making decisions about how to respond to an email, what to say on the phone or how to prioritise your work can seem overwhelming at the end of a long day, or even at the start.

Research suggests that mindfulness training has a number of positive effects on decision-making, such as improving the quality of information you consider when you make decisions, recognising ethical challenges and reducing con-firmation bias, which is the tendency to look for evidence to support what you already believe. Mindfulness also helps to reduce the tendency to be blinded by experience, which in turn allows you to respond creatively.

A quiet mind makes better decisions. Without the mental frenzy, you're able to see more clearly what, if anything, needs to be done and whether a decision is, in fact, required. Over the past few years mindfulness has helped me to notice my tendency to over-consult when decisions need to be made. Nowadays, I find myself gathering fewer opinions and spending less time dwelling, regretting and ruminating over what might have been, or how I feel I should respond. In turn this helps me to preserve my limited pot of energy.

The Practice: The next time you're faced with having to make a difficult decision, see if you can engage your mindfulness practice by focusing on your breath or sensations that arise in your body. As you weigh the factors which impact on your ability to decide, pay attention to any outside influences that you become aware of. Take time to consider what is influencing your decision-making and whether or not these factors are habitual, stem from anxiety, or reflect your core beliefs and values.

Consider: How might you reduce decision-fatigue in your workplace? Perhaps you could start by reducing mental distraction, which often requires the making of lots of small decisions. Consider switching off notifications, single-tasking rather than multitasking and becoming more aware of whether or not the demands that are placed on you actually require a decision to be made.

Dealing with Difficult Colleagues

Over forty workplace research studies have linked mindfulness to improved relationships, better collaboration and greater employee resilience.[29] So how could mindfulness help you to deal with difficult colleagues at work?

When someone acts unpleasantly, it's often hard to feel any compassion towards them. You may feel resentful or angry and withdraw, or choose to confront. Practising mindfulness helps you to pause, recognise and label strong feelings as they arise. By doing so, you buy yourself a moment to soften your response and create a possibility for greater connection, rather than a knee-jerk reaction. At the very least you become more able to let go of feelings of anger or resentment.

The Practice: The next time you feel challenged by the difficult behaviour of a colleague, see if you can notice any strong feelings that arise. Pause, breathe and allow them to pass before considering how to handle the situation with kindness to yourself. See whether this makes a difference to how you feel and how your colleague responds.

A similar approach is known as the S.T.O.P practice: S – Stop whatever you are doing, T – Take three deep breaths, O – Observe how your body feels, and P – Proceed with kindness and compassion to yourself.

HOME

Being Curious

Being curious is an essential attitude of mindfulness, which encourages us to turn towards our entire experience, however difficult it may be. With mindfulness, there is less jumping to conclusions and more opening up to the richness and complexity of life.

Curiosity also allows us to explore relationships mindfully – to see people afresh rather than through the lens of role, title, position, or impression of how they fit, or don't fit in. This involves a crucial shift from thinking about the experience to being *in* the experience.

The Practice: Being curious leads to new connections. See what difference it makes when you bring an attitude of curiosity to your work and relationships with your colleagues, family and friends. Talk to someone new at the school gate, speak with a stranger as you travel to work, or ask a friend about her aspirations for the year ahead. Lean in and seek out common humanity by simply being curious.

HOME

Single-tasking

Research from Stanford University in the US shows that the concept of multitasking is a myth.[30] What people are actually doing when they're trying to multitask is task-switching, which is where your attention constantly flicks from one thing to another. This process of switching diminishes performance. So in the rush to get things done, it seems that many of us have lost the more effective ability to 'single task'. Is it possible then to slow down and become more productive?

The Practice: See if you can reduce or stop multitasking and notice how it feels to tackle one job at a time. You can use this practice at home or at work. Try putting household admin tasks together and completing them one at a time, such as paying bills, cleaning, sorting out school clubs and organising food for the week. Move on next to life affirming or creative activities that require a different field of your attention, such as playing with your child, being with friends or practising your latest hobby, whether it's gardening, origami or opera. Notice how this impacts on your productivity and ability to focus.

Bring your attention purposefully to any pleasurable moments that arise throughout the day, dropping any expectations you may have for them, and giving your full attention to each in turn. It may be a conversation with a friend or simply making dinner. Slow down and notice how it feels.

* MINDFULNESS MEDITATION *

The Body Scan

This meditation invites you to bring your attention to different parts of the body in sequence, without judgment. The practice allows you to identify what you are feeling and where you are feeling it. Use your body as an anchor to your present moment experience and listen to the body scan meditation.

A QUICK REMINDER

+ Your fight-flight-freeze stress response can be triggered by worry and anxiety. Practising mindfulness meditation acts as a counterbalance to the stress response by engaging your 'rest and digest' parasympathetic nervous system. This enables your heart rate to slow, blood pressure to reduce, circulation to improve and your digestion to normalise.

+ With mindfulness, you can change the way you relate to fear and approach it with awareness, openness and curiosity, rather than avoiding it or pushing it away.

+ When you find yourself overthinking, ruminating or catastrophising, try the simple practice of saying 'stop' before taking a few deep breaths.

+ If closing your eyes to meditate creates anxiety or fearfulness, meditate with your eyes open, using a soft, unfocused gaze.

+ If you become aware of aches and pains when you meditate, you may want to adjust your posture or position. Alternatively, simply notice the ache, breathe into that area and continue.

CHAPTER 5

RESILIENCE, SLEEP AND KINDNESS TO SELF

When I started to practise mindfulness meditation, it was important for me to understand how and why it works. The growing body of scientific research fascinated me and I wanted to know more about the impact of mindfulness on daily life. This chapter explores the relationship between mindfulness and resilience, how the practice might help you to get a better night's sleep, and the all-important concept of self-compassion.

RESILIENCE

Resilience is the ability to adapt and bounce back in the face of stress and adversity. It prevents you from disappearing down a black hole, folding in and giving up when things go wrong. It moves you from passive to active, from victim to warrior – or somewhere in-between. Resilience is the grit that helps you to get up and carry on in the hope that things will get better. It's the capacity to adjust positively to difficult life circumstances.

'If you tell me why the fen appears impassable, I then will tell you why I think that I can get across it if I try.'

Marianne Moore

Psychologist and resilience expert Boris Cyrulnik describes resilience as a sweater you knit yourself 'using the people and things [you] meet in [y]our emotional and social environments.'[31] Resilience is multidimensional and is made up of genetics, epigenetics (the switching of genes on and off), your environment, social factors and how the circuits in your brain wire together.[32] Research suggests that resilience is predicted by your ability to manage stress.[33] Importantly, it is capable of being strengthened.

So what does resilience feel like? Author and psychologist Rick Hanson describes it as an 'unshakable core of well-being', characterised by strength, calm and happiness.[34] We all need some degree of resilience to progress at work, raise children, overcome illness and pursue personal goals and ambitions.

So does mindfulness have a role to play in building resilience? As a practice, we know that it enhances our ability to cope with stressful events by bringing our attention towards our immediate experience. This approach helps us to appreciate the transient nature of our thoughts and refrain from over-evaluating them. We become more flexible in our responses and better able to regulate our emotions, particularly the difficult ones.

It's true that some people rebound more quickly than others when something bad happens, and in recent years neuroscientists have started to measure this recovery time. One study found that mindful people cope better with difficult thoughts and emotions and are less likely to become overwhelmed or to shut down emotionally.[35] Another study showed that mindfulness is a significant predictor of resilience.[36]

Although research in this area is still at an early stage, indicators of a relationship between mindfulness and resilience are encouraging. I know that a regular mindfulness practice helps me to create a sense of space between what happens on a day-to-day basis and how I am able to respond. With mindfulness, there is less risk of getting sucked in, carried away, or driven to distraction by negative thoughts or emotions. It helps me to see things more clearly and to be able to move forward in the midst of life's inevitable challenges. These significant benefits of mindfulness complement the central core of resilience, which is the ability to navigate change.

SLEEP

Insomnia is a massive public health problem and the most commonly reported mental health complaint in the UK, affecting up to one-third of the population.[37] Most people have experienced how a night without proper sleep can ruin an entire day. You feel tired, uninspired and ready for a fight. It affects your mood, energy and concentration levels. It can also impact your relationships, ability to function at work and often goes hand-in-hand with depression and anxiety. People who don't get enough sleep are at a far greater risk of heart disease or stroke, compared to those who sleep for seven or eight hours each night. Sleep loss causes a significant decrease in creativity, divergent thinking, decision-making, short-term and working memory.[38]

A study in the US found that more than a third of workers got less than the recommended seven hours of sleep per night.[39] In the UK, a survey conducted in 2017 found that three-quarters of Brits cited workplace stress as a key cause of their disrupted sleep, with more than 90 per cent admitting that stress-related disrupted sleep negatively affects their emotions.[40] Lack of sleep costs the US up to $411 billion a year, followed by Japan (up to $138 billion a year), Germany (up to $60 billion) and the UK (up to $50 billion).[41]

Ultimately, sleep is crucial for restoring your body and mind. It's when the brain does most of its development and repair work. So how does mindfulness meditation affect sleep?

Research in this area is growing and a number of reports suggest positive links between mindfulness meditation and improved quality of sleep. In one study, a group of older adults learned various mindfulness techniques, which they practised for two hours a week. At the end of six weeks, researchers measured the sleep quality of all participants – those who tried mindfulness meditation and those who learned a standard sleep hygiene education programme. They found that the group practising mindfulness scored higher. The study's author explained that people who can't sleep often start to worry, which prevents them from being able to get back to sleep. With mindfulness, people learn how to observe their thoughts, without elaborating on them. Acquiring this skill helps them to drift off to sleep more easily.[42] Researchers have also found that mindfulness meditation can help those who struggle with chronic insomnia.[43]

So what can you do to get yourself back to sleep if you wake in the middle of the night? One simple practice is to see if you can follow the passage of just one breath, and then another – one at a time. As you do this, keeping your attention focused on your breath as best you can, you will activate the parasympathetic nervous system, which should help you to drift back off to sleep. Alternatively, you could try using a mantra, such as 'Breathing in I am calm, Breathing out, all is well'. Repeating this short

'Sleep is as important to our health as eating, drinking and breathing. It allows our bodies to repair themselves and our brains to consolidate our memories and process information.'

Mental Health Foundation

refrain silently to yourself will give the mind a point of focus and should slow the pace of racing thoughts.

Practising a short body-scan practice can also help. If you wake in the night, distract your mind away from worrying by asking it instead to scan your body. Begin by bringing your attention to your toes and work your way up to the top of your head. By the time I get to my shoulders, I am usually fast asleep.

You could also try a visualisation practice, where you picture in your mind a place of safety. It might be somewhere that is either known to you or a figment of your imagination. Invite the mind to spend time recreating the detail of your location – the weather, the foliage, the view and the surroundings. It might be a beach scene with gentle waves lapping on the sand, a cool forest, or a mountain vista. By inviting the mind to imagine the scene, you steer it away from anxious thoughts that might otherwise keep you awake.

The ability to activate your 'rest and digest' nervous system by practising mindfulness meditation is a useful tool for inducing sleep and improving its quality. Try the 'single breath' practice, reciting a simple mantra, a body scan or visualisation the next time you're unable to get back to sleep.

CASE STUDY: IMPROVING SLEEP

In one study, participants with no formal meditation training were given reading materials that introduced them to mindfulness. They received instructions and guided meditations for four specific mindfulness practices: a three-minute 'mindful breathing' exercise (which focused attention on the breath), the body scan (moving focus across different areas of the body), mindfully focusing on an everyday task (such as preparing breakfast or taking a shower), and loving-kindness meditation (sending feelings of love and compassion to themselves and others).

Over the course of two weeks, the participants were asked to meditate using these practices for ten minutes each day before and after work. In addition, the participants completed a series of questions in the morning, at the end of work and at bedtime to track their sleep quality, amount of mindfulness at work, and their ability to detach from work-related thoughts after coming home.

The results showed that over the course of the two-week period, the meditators experienced steady improvements in sleep quality, sleep duration and mindfulness, but did not demonstrate significant enhancements in their ability to detach from work. The report's author explained that: 'It is likely you would have to train more intensely or for longer periods of time before you see any effects on psychological detachment ... but it is possible that sleep quality is more sensitive to meditation and that you see the positive effects of the mindfulness training earlier.' The report's author explained that ultimately: 'Mindfulness is not something that you can just train properly in one or two weeks ... If you want sustainable effects, you have to keep practicing regularly.'[44]

SELF-COMPASSION

Self-compassion is a radical practice that changes the way you relate to yourself. Dr Kristen Neff, a leading researcher in this field, describes it as the ability to meet reality with kindness to yourself. While you may be adept at giving kindness to others, when was the last time

'If your compassion does not include yourself, it is incomplete.'

Jack Kornfield

'Talking to ourselves in a very un-compassionate, self-critical way, is rarely helpful. Interrupt these self-attacking trains of thought by asking quietly, "How does this help me?" You'll see straight away that beating yourself up usually gets you nowhere.'

Padraig O'Morain

you gave it to yourself and truly considered your own needs? You might even struggle to know what it means to be kind to yourself. In physical terms, it might be as simple as a hot bath, drinking a good cup of coffee, going to bed when you've got a cold, saying 'no' to a social engagement, reading a novel, taking a taxi, having a moment of quiet, or simply being alone. Self compassion is the ability to give yourself the advice you would give to a good friend who is having a hard time.

The idea of becoming your own best friend sounds simple, yet in reality, it takes practice. Self-compassion involves giving yourself the friendly, supportive advice you need to stop the self-criticism that emerges when you're up against it. When you are kind to yourself, you recognise your own suffering rather than beating yourself up or moving straight into problem-solving mode.

I remember exactly where I was sat in my local village hall when my mindfulness teacher explained the concept of self-compassion. Perhaps I was naïve but I had never thought about it prior to that moment, and yet what she said made sense and gave me the language to express what I had been trying to do, often in vain, when things went wrong.

Unfortunately, self-compassion is not widely taught in schools, universities or the workplace and yet its power to help heal is undeniable. Research on the ability of self-compassion to boost one's sense of well-being and provide longer-term health benefits is growing rapidly as the concept takes hold. Self-compassion asks you to stop, notice and recognise that this moment is difficult, for whatever reason. Acknowledging the difficulty helps you to tune in to what you need. It emboldens your courage and strengthens your resilience to carry on.

CASE STUDY: LOVING KINDNESS

One study found that just seven minutes of loving-kindness practice boosts a person's good feelings and sense of social connection, if only temporarily.[45]

Neff explains that there are three core components to self-compassion. The first is being kind to yourself, rather than self-critical. The second is to recognise the common humanity of suffering – namely that we're all in it together and that we all suffer, albeit in different ways. Acknowledging the messy business of being human and the imperfection of life brings people together and breaks down a sense of isolation that often arises in times of crisis. It also reduces the tendency for over-identification, where you become so absorbed by your own emotional experience that you're unable to step outside yourself and gain the perspective you need to understand the shared nature of suffering.[46] The third component is mindfulness, the state of moment-to-moment awareness, which asks you to notice your suffering and how it makes you feel, however hard it may be, rather than pushing it away or denying its existence. Often people don't even realise that they are suffering or acknowledge that things are tough. Mindfulness asks you to recognise the difficulty and gives you the space to question whether what you think is actually true. It helps to prevent overreactions and unnecessary confrontations.

Self-compassion has been described as the emotional heart of mindfulness, but how do the two concepts relate to one another in practice? Neff explains that with mindfulness, you accept the experience that arises. With self-compassion, you care *for* the experience. With mindfulness, the focus is on the question 'What am I experiencing right now?', whereas with self-compassion, the question changes to 'What do I need right now?' When you are mindful of your difficulties, you feel your suffering with spacious awareness. When you are self-compassionate, you are kind to yourself when you suffer.[47] Unlike self-esteem, which can go up and down depending upon how you rate your own self-worth at any particular given moment, self-compassion can be practised regardless of your circumstances. It's not tied up with how you perceive your future career or social standing and whether or not you're above average when compared to your colleagues, friends and family. Treating yourself with self-compassion is available, no matter what, even when your self-esteem has taken a serious battering. Self-compassion doesn't involve judging yourself. Rather, it's a way of relating to the challenges you face with kindness and it develops naturally from practising mindfulness.

Many people think they need to criticise themselves and their performance to keep motivated, but in fact, research shows that excessive self-criticism undermines self-confidence. It leads to a greater fear of failure and triggers your fight-flight-freeze stress response. Sometimes the

'Mindfulness and self-compassion form a state of warm-hearted, connected presence that strengthens us during difficult moments in our lives.'

Dr Kristen Neff

sting of self-criticism can be so intense that it stops you from learning or pursuing your goals. With self-compassion, you acknowledge your own shortcomings in a way that is constructive, with kindness, which means you're more likely to be able to see the changes you want to make in the future.

Some may argue that self-compassion is self-indulgent, but in fact research shows that it leads to long-term health benefits and healthier behaviours, such as exercising, drinking less alcohol and eating well.[48] Greater self-compassion is also linked to less anxiety and depression,[49] greater joy and happiness, feelings of social connectedness and life satisfaction.[50] One study found that practising seven weeks of loving-kindness meditation increased love, joy, contentment, gratitude, pride, hope, interest, amusement and awe.[51] Another study showed that loving-kindness meditation was effective in reducing self-criticism and depressive symptoms, while improving self-compassion and positive emotions.[52]

In practical terms, it involves the bringing of a friendly, caring attitude towards yourself. For me, it's about taking a break when I need one, going for a walk on my own, phoning a friend and carving out the time to exercise and eat well. It's about using a voice of kindness and understanding towards myself when difficulties arise.

Ultimately, self-compassion is about tuning in to what you need and recognising difficulty, anxiety and pain when it arises. It's a leaning in, rather than a pushing away. It's about engaging your natural response to suffering, as you would with a friend in trouble, and being kind to yourself when you need it most.

FREQUENTLY ASKED QUESTIONS

WHAT DO I DO IF A WORRY ARISES WHILE I'M MEDITATING?

When we worry, our normal tendency is to try to find a solution. Yet this can often produce feelings of anxiety, particularly if an answer is not immediately forthcoming. Instead of getting obsessed with finding an answer, perhaps you can allow the worry to come and go using mindfulness. During your meditation practice, it's not uncommon for worries to surface. If this happens, see if you can notice where you feel the worry in your body. Notice also any linked thoughts that might accompany the worry, and resist the temptation to follow or cling on to them. Label the worry if it helps, for example 'worrying about paying the mortgage', 'worrying about my dad's health' or 'worrying about the deadline next week'. Then see if you can return to your point of anchor, allowing the worry to pass. This practice of returning the mind to the present moment prevents any unnecessary fuelling of the original worry and allows you to stand back slightly in order to assess what you really need to do in order to feel better.

CASE STUDY: WORKING MEMORY

Five studies on working memory showed that the average meditator has a better working memory than sixty-two per cent of non-meditators.[53]

IF I MEDITATE, WILL I LOSE 'MY EDGE'?

As a criminal barrister, I wondered what my colleagues might think once they knew I meditated and practised mindfulness. I was curious about whether I might be perceived as having lost my 'combative edge' or as somehow weak. It took me at least six months to grapple with these feelings, which I'm reassured by a colleague who has been meditating for thirty years, is no time at all.

On reflection, I knew that my mindfulness practice had improved my performance as a lawyer. I became a better listener, I was more self-aware and more compassionate. Once I started to share it with others, I realised that many of my colleagues either practised some form of meditation already or were keen to do so. Rather than lose my 'edge', I gained a platform from which to speak openly about some of the professional challenges we face and how mindfulness might help us to respond to at least some of them.

ISN'T MEDITATION SELF-INDULGENT?

When you meditate, you learn about where your mind likes to wander. You spend time cultivating the qualities of patience, acceptance, awareness, forgiveness and empathy. This self-awareness helps you to understand the behaviour of others and to forge more resilient relationships. It's a life skill that empowers you to be more present with those you love and those you work alongside. To conclude, learning to meditate is far from self-indulgent.

DAILY MINDFULNESS

The daily mindfulness practices in this chapter focus on listening and the benefit of setting reminders to practise, even just for a few minutes. There's also advice on how to bring mindfulness to your driving experience.

WORKPLACE

Mindful Listening

Listening is an art. But how often do you really listen to what your colleague, boss, friend or loved one is saying? Even if you consider yourself to be a 'good listener', do you really tune in with your body and mind to what is being said?

The psychologist Albert Mehrabian's communication model explains that only seven per cent of what is communicated consists of the content of the message. The use of voice, tone, intonation and volume make up thirty-eight per cent and as much as fifty-five per cent of communication is body language.[54] So how much do we miss by not fully tuning in?

Given that our normal tendency is to fill in the gaps, assume we know the point and express our views before the other person has finished their sentence, consider if you can pause and take a moment to really listen.

The Practice: This practice requires that when you're listening, you listen. Don't do anything else. Lean in, give appropriate eye contact and refrain from formulating your own response before you have heard what is being said. Be fully present. Notice the speaker's voice, tone, intonation, volume and body language. Pause and allow the person to finish. Communicate clearly and be aware of the possible effect of your words on those around you. See what difference it makes.

'Most people do not listen with the intent to understand; they listen with the intent to reply'

– Stephen R Covey

Setting Mindful Reminders

One of the greatest challenges of mindfulness is remembering to practise! It's easy to be drawn back into the default mode of getting lost in thoughts and running away with your own narrative, usually with a negative slant. Having a few reminders around the house and at your workplace to prompt you to be mindful can help keep your new habit on track.

The Practice: Set some reminders at home and at work. You may want to use a Post-it note, an inspiring quote or a gentle bell on your phone that rings several times a day. Use these alerts to remind you to take a few mindful breaths, wherever you are.

Mindful Driving

Driving can be both pleasurable and highly stressful. It is sometimes a means to an end, carried out in semi-automatic pilot mode, where you arrive at your destination without being fully aware of how you got there. Buildings, landscapes, signposts and turnings disappear as you travel headlong towards your destination.

Traffic jams and road rage are commonplace and can trigger your fight-flight-freeze stress response. Is it possible as you set off on your journey today to bring a more mindful approach to your driving experience?

The Practice: The next time you're stuck in heavy traffic, waiting at the traffic lights or you feel road rage rising, see if you can use this time as an opportunity to practise mindfulness. Turn off the radio, follow your natural breath, feel the steering wheel and notice your surroundings. If you're moving in slow traffic, look around and notice the faces of others caught up in the same situation. Some may be stressed and angry, others may be singing along to the radio, chatting or laughing.

Can you bring a light touch, a sense of kindness or even a smile to your driving predicament, no matter how challenging it may seem?

HOME

The Chocolate Practice

I tried this mindfulness practice some years ago with a group of students at my local youth centre. They didn't want to meditate or spend time learning about it, yet when they heard that chocolate was involved, five of them volunteered. At the end of the practice, they shared insights about their experience and stories about bullying and loneliness at school. It felt as though this short time out together had given them a space and the opportunity to connect over things that mattered, even if only momentarily.

This practice is an exercise in mindful eating which involves paying full attention to the experience, both inside and outside your body. Its purpose is to help you connect to your senses and so enable you to drop into the present moment.

The Practice: Choose a piece of chocolate: dark, white, milk, whichever you prefer. Open the packet and inhale the scent. Break off a piece and examine its edges, imperfections and texture. Put the piece in your mouth and see if it's possible to let it rest on your tongue without biting into it. See if you can let it melt and notice the experience. If your attention wanders away from the chocolate, gently bring it back, noticing where it has wandered to. Once it has melted, swallow the chocolate and consider how this practice differs from the way in which you normally eat your favourite bar.

* MINDFULNESS MEDITATION *

Arising Sounds and Thoughts Meditation

Both sounds and thoughts appear as if from nowhere and are capable of triggering powerful emotions. This guided open-monitoring meditation will help you to understand how you can relate to unsettling thoughts. Let thoughts, sounds, feelings and sensations come and go — without getting carried away with what you think they represent. Listen to the arising sounds and thoughts meditation.

A QUICK REMINDER

✦ Resilience is the ability to adapt and bounce back in the face of stress or adversity. Research has shown that individuals with higher mindfulness have greater resilience.

✦ Insomnia can affect your mood, energy and concentration levels. Research suggests positive links between the practice of mindfulness meditation and improved sleep quality.

✦ Self-compassion has three core elements: (1) being kind to yourself, (2) recognising the common humanity of suffering, and (3) mindfulness. Unlike self-esteem, which can go up and down depending on how you rate your own self-worth, self-compassion can be practised regardless of your circumstances.

✦ It's not uncommon for worries to surface during a meditation. Notice any linked thoughts that might accompany the worry. Resist the temptation to follow or cling on to them and return to your point of anchor, allowing the worry to pass.

✦ By practising mindfulness meditation, you're not at risk of losing your 'edge' or becoming complacent. Spending time learning to meditate isn't self-indulgent. It's a life skill that enables you to be more present.

CHAPTER 6

FIGHTS, HABITS AND MOVING ON

This final chapter deals with managing conflict and breaking bad habits. There are also some tips and advice on how to maintain your new practice in the weeks and months ahead, with more answers to frequently asked questions.

MANAGING CONFLICT

Conflict is an innate and vital part of life. While being constantly on alert is not healthy, many people feel the stress of conflict every day, to a greater or lesser degree. People fall out, disagree and feel affronted. It's easy to become embroiled in arguing with colleagues, clients and even your children, on an almost daily basis.

Everyone deals with conflict differently and many have learned to identify the triggers that set them off. Even so, it can be hard to find a way of tackling conflict productively without undermining your sense of self. Adopting a mindful approach to strife is easier said than done. As a war crimes barrister and as a mother, I came to mindfulness out of pure need – to enable me to be more present, less reactive and to make better decisions. Conflict has always been a natural part of my professional working life, but knowing when to walk away and when to engage is something I still struggle with, although mindfulness helps.

When a conflict arises, the practice reminds you to approach it non-judgmentally. Rather than lashing out, you can choose to pause, take a moment and breathe slowly which helps you to assess how to respond. Mindfulness reminds you to refrain from leaping to assumptions you might otherwise make. While it's easy to attribute motive to another's actions, if you're able to leave judgment aside, you have a chance of seeing the situation for what it really is, rather than what you think it's about. It also helps you to take disputes less personally in the first place.

One of the great benefits of mindfulness is its ability to repair the *consequences* of conflict. This doesn't necessarily mean that you argue less, but rather that you do it with greater awareness and empathy for the other's point of view. You become more willing to accept that everyone falls prey to strong emotions, such as anger, pride or jealousy. You are less attached to the emotions themselves and therefore more willing to work on the heart of the disagreement.

For my part, I find that I'm less likely to judge and more likely to listen, which dramatically alters my personal experience of discord both in the workplace and at home. It also helps me to forgive others (and myself) more quickly and to acknowledge that conflict is an inevitable part of life. It's how we handle it that matters.

BREAKING BAD HABITS

Whether it's checking your email every few minutes, restlessly searching the internet for a new home you can't afford, overeating, drinking too much, smoking or spending too long grazing on social media sites, everyone has at least two bad habits they would like to break. But why is it so hard and why does willpower fail you when you need it most?

In his TED talk, 'A Simple Way to Break a Bad Habit', psychiatrist Judson Brewer explains that the brain follows the pattern of 'trigger, behaviour, reward – repeat'.[55] When you feel stressed, you might reach for a drink, your favourite sweets or a cigarette, which seem to make you feel better momentarily. Then you repeat the process and a habit starts to form. It's the emotional trigger of feeling sad, bad, tired or in need which leads to the bad habit.

In his research on one habit in particular, Brewer and his colleagues found that mindfulness training could help people to stop smoking. The group of participants had already tried and failed to quit smoking before, on average six times. The study found that mindfulness was twice as effective at helping people to stop, when compared with the 'Freedom from Smoking' programme in the US. Brewer explains that the mindfulness training helped the smokers to become curious about their experience. Rather than being asked to stop smoking, they were encouraged to taste, smell and register how it really made them feel. This awareness of their experience and curiosity led them to becoming disenchanted with their habit and led to a realisation 'in their bones' that they did not want to continue. It was this disenchantment that helped the participants let go of their habitual behaviour and move from 'knowledge to wisdom'.

Even though your thinking brain, the pre-frontal cortex, knows it's bad to smoke, or antisocial to text during dinner, and does everything it can to stop it, Brewer explains that this part of the brain goes offline when you get tired or stressed. The reality is that you just can't stop yourself from yelling at your children or grabbing a cigarette, even though you know this is not how you want to behave. You fall back into old habits and lose what is known as 'cognitive control'.

This is where mindfulness can help. Rather than getting sucked in by physical cravings, you notice their arrival and allow them to fall away of their own accord. Getting up close and personal with your own bad habits reveals how little they actually serve you. It's with this realisation and a growing sense of disenchantment that you become able to extricate yourself from their grip. When you're curious about your experience, it helps you step outside your entrenched behaviour. One theory as to how mindfulness works is that a region of the brain (known as the 'posterior cingulate cortex') is activated by cravings. Yet when we bring our awareness towards the cravings and become curious about them (for example, by tasting and feeling the smoke) activity in this brain area reduces, which helps us to break the habit.

So the next time a craving hits, whether it's food, alcohol, smoking or incessant email checking, why not follow Brewer's advice and notice the intensity of the urge, get curious about it, feel the joy of letting go – *and repeat.*

MAINTAINING MINDFULNESS

Part of the challenge of mindfulness is remembering to find the time to practise, *no matter what.* While the average human being takes around 20,000 breaths every day, paying attention to just a tiny fraction of these can be difficult. As you reach the end of this book, take a moment to reflect on your mindfulness journey so far. What challenges have you faced and how have you overcome them? Which practices have you enjoyed? Which have proved to be more tricky, and why? Have you been able to bring some mindfulness into your daily life at work and at home? Which aspects do you want to continue? If you have used the mindfulness and gratitude log at the back of the book, how helpful has it been in supporting your practice?

Perhaps you have already started to experience some of the benefits of mindfulness? As you continue, consider how you might find support in the weeks and months ahead. Is there a quiet workspace you can claim or a colleague you can share your experience with? Some companies now encourage employees to meet for mindful lunches, go on silent walks, or support regular practice groups where people can meditate together. Consider how your workplace might help you to support the building of a wider mindfulness initiative.

At some point along the way, you can expect to hit a brick wall, fall by the wayside, feel that you don't have time to meditate, or that you're just not 'cut out for it'. At these moments, when you struggle to continue, rather than viewing it as a sign that you should give up, take a self-compassionate attitude and consider what you need to do to get your practice back on track, rather than abandon it altogether. Reflect on the benefits you have reaped and how you can seek to maintain your mindfulness in a way that works for you.

FREQUENTLY ASKED QUESTIONS

MY PARTNER/SON/FRIEND NEEDS MINDFULNESS – HOW DO I PERSUADE THEM TO TRY IT?

One of the best ways to 'persuade' others to try mindfulness is to tend to the quality of your own practice first. Leading by example and demonstrating in your daily life how mindfulness helps you may persuade others to want to learn more. You could also refer them to the scientifically proven benefits, which provide powerful evidence as to the impact that a regular practice can have on different aspects of daily life. Even if you feel that they need it more than you do, your own mindfulness will inevitably influence their lives, so just keep going!

IS MINDFULNESS JUST A FAD?

No. Meditation practices that use mindfulness have existed for thousands of years. More recently, in the late 1970s, an eight-week mindfulness course, known as 'Mindfulness-Based Stress Reduction' (MBSR) was developed by Dr Jon Kabat-Zinn at the

University of Massachusetts Medical School to treat patients struggling with chronic pain. This marked the introduction of secular mindfulness. Over 750 medical centres in the US now offer MBSR programmes with courses being taught around the world, in hospitals and clinics, schools and businesses. In the 1990s, Mindfulness-Based Cognitive Therapy (MBCT) was developed by Zindel Segal, Mark Williams and John Teasdale, a programme for people at risk of relapse into depression. More generally, scientific research on the mental, physical and emotional benefits of mindfulness continues to grow with the publication of a large number of peer-reviewed research papers each year.

DAILY MINDFULNESS

The ability to tune in to others and use positivity and optimism are explored in these final daily mindfulness practices. There is also an opportunity for you to transform a household chore into a mindful moment.

WORKPLACE

Tuning in to Others

How often do you ask someone the question 'How are you?' only to trail off or look away before hearing the answer? How often have you spent time with colleagues, friends or even family members where you have come away from a conversation feeling a sense of disconnect, mistrust or resentment because you were ignored, judged or not listened to? People are often so driven by tales of their own experience that they forget to tune in to those around them. They miss out on the pleasure of connection, the coincidences that might have been uncovered and the questions they could have asked, if only they had truly listened. They lose the opportunity to empathise, share, console or congratulate, as time is taken up with measuring what they heard and how it affects their self-worth. Under pressure from social media, even the present moment is busy being edited to show only the good bits – the extravagance, the beauty and expense.

The Practice: When you start work today and have your first conversation with colleagues, customers or friends, see if you can tune in to their experience, problem, delight, concern or joy. Notice how this connection evolves and how it feels. See how it differs from your usual interactions and how the other person responds. If it's helpful, write down your observations in the mindfulness and gratitude log.

WORKPLACE
Optimism and Positivity

Over time, it's easy to become complacent or even cynical about aspects of your work and even your colleagues. Negative experiences of being let down, made redundant or betrayed, can lead to vulnerability or overprotectiveness, as you remain on alert waiting for things to go wrong. This way of being feels restrictive, but it's hard to shake in times of uncertainty.

So how might you change your outlook and drop any negative assumptions you may harbour? What could mindfulness have to offer in terms of how you approach your work and your colleagues?

With practice, mindfulness allows you to tune in to the subtlety of your experience. You become more able to be present to whatever's going on and better able to navigate choppy waters, in the knowledge that this cannot last for ever. With practice, mindfulness helps you to become kinder to yourself, more forgiving to others and better able to give both people and situations the benefit of the doubt. You start to acknowledge your fears and become curious about them, rather than accepting them as facts about yourself. You then have the option to choose to bring a positive, optimistic outlook to the day ahead, which research has shown is linked to longevity and even helps people to cope better with illness. Such an attitiude can also enable you to spot opportunities, foster better social interaction, contribute more proactively and generate positive feelings.

The Practice: Take a moment to consider how you feel about your workplace and your colleagues. Notice any negative feelings or sensations that arise. See if you can encourage an attitude of positivity and optimism and notice how this impacts on the course of your day and on those around you.

HOME

A Mindful Chore

Is it possible to be mindful when doing a household chore that you might otherwise rush through mindlessly or complete reluctantly? Can you use this time productively to de-stress your mind and body in order to feel better about a task you dislike?

The Practice: At some point this week, whether it's the ironing, cleaning the bathroom or emptying the dishwasher, select a household chore you would rather avoid. Choose the one you dislike the most and see if you can set aside time to complete it, without feeling rushed. Notice the detail of the chore, the impact of finishing it and how you feel as you go along.

Use this time as an opportunity to breathe and slow down. How does the bringing of a mindful attitude compare with your normal way of getting this job done? Now consider how you could use this approach in other areas of your daily life.

'Don't do any task
in order to get it over
with. Resolve to do each job
in a relaxed way, with all your
attention. Enjoy and be one
with your work.'

Thich Nhat Hanh

HOME

Crowds, Queues and Delays

It is normal to feel frustrated or annoyed when you don't get a seat on the train, when you have to queue at the supermarket, when you're stuck in traffic or squeezed on a bus on your way to work. These logistical challenges often arise before the day has truly begun. Nerves have been frayed, patience tested and energy depleted before your 'To Do' list has been located, let alone consulted.

But what if you could use each of these events as moments to practise mindfulness? What if you could decide not to rise to the occasion but to recognise the difficulty of the situation, breathe and accept it as it is?

The Practice: How could you transform a frenetic, infuriating, or irritating experience into an opportunity to activate your parasympathetic nervous system and feel better? Rather than turning a minor hitch into an energy-draining drama, the next time you're confronted by a crowd, queue or delay, consider how you could approach it more mindfully.

Perhaps try this 'RAIN' practice, the acronym for which was first coined twenty years ago by meditation teacher Michele McDonald.[56] It stands for (R)ecognise, (A)llow, (I)nvestigate and (N)on-identify.

The first step involves (R)ecognising what is happening in the moment and how it makes you feel, for example 'This traffic jam is really annoying and is a waste of my time'. It sounds straightforward but most of us move into reaction and blame mode first, rather than simply taking stock. **The second step** involves (A)ccepting. This doesn't mean that you're OK with the situation that has arisen. Rather it means that you acknowledge and name what is happening. For example, 'I feel really angry and annoyed!' **The third step** is about (I)nvestigating the sensations that arise in your body. It involves physically noticing where the emotions have landed. Is there a feeling of tightness, contraction, pain, a flush of energy, or a quickened heart beat? Feel the emotion that has been triggered by the thought and take time to breathe, allowing the feelings and sensations to pass. Investigate with kindness to yourself without probing too deeply. **The last step** is about (N)on-identification with what has arisen. There's no need to add a 'me' element into it or turn it into a vulnerability or weakness. Observe what arose as a bystander, rather than over-identifying with it, and move on.

* LOVING KINDNESS MEDITATION *

For the final practice, I have chosen a loving kindness meditation. As you will recall from Chapter 5, compassion helps us to mend relationships and move forward, while fostering a sense of well-being. In this practice, let your mind rest in the compassionate phrases you hear, which will be the focus of your attention. Listen to the loving kindness meditation.

A QUICK REMINDER

✦ By bringing a sense of compassion and empathy to your experience of conflict, you become more willing to accept that everyone falls prey to strong emotions, such as anger, pride or jealousy.

✦ By using mindfulness to get up close and personal with your bad habits, you may start to see how little they actually serve you.

✦ To maintain your mindfulness practice, consider joining or setting up a group at work where you can share your experience with others. Think about how your workplace might support you.

✦ If you pause, stop or struggle with your mindfulness practice, try to view it through the lens of self-compassion to see what you need to do for yourself in order to return and begin again.

✦ Demonstrating in your daily life how mindfulness helps you may persuade others to try it for themselves.

✦ Mindfulness is not a fad. Meditation practices that use mindfulness have existed for thousands of years.

CONCLUSION

Learning to practise mindfulness is not just about finding five or ten minutes each day to sit and meditate. It's much more than that. It's about developing awareness, patience, a non-judgmental attitude and compassion for yourself and others. It's about knowing when you're at risk of being taken prisoner by your own emotions and judging when and how to respond. It's about tuning in, listening, giving the benefit of the doubt, forgiveness, and living more in the present moment before it's gone.

If you continue to practise in the weeks, months and years ahead, I hope you will find that gradually mindfulness will seep into your way of being – at least for some parts of the day. You will become mindful of when you're not mindful and more able to detach yourself from overthinking and taking self-critical thoughts seriously.

I am confident that a sustained practice will lead you towards a calmer way of life. This doesn't mean that you will become visibly Zen, or never lose your temper. It does mean, however, that you might worry less and care more. Developing a mindful approach might just change the entire course of your life.

A 14-DAY MINDFULNESS AND GRATITUDE LOG

When you start meditating, it's useful to keep a log of what you have been practising, as it can motivate you to carry on. This mindfulness and gratitude log has been designed to help you record your journey. Write down the type of meditation you practised or listened to, its duration and where you meditated. Note down the challenges you faced and the app you used, if applicable. See if you can also record your daily mindfulness practices, whether it's making a cup of tea, taking a bath or preparing your favourite food.

Use the gratitude entry to record three things you feel grateful for, either at the start or end of each day. See how this practice makes you feel. Consider if it's something you want to continue beyond the fourteen days. Your log doesn't have to be detailed, but keeping a note might encourage you to carry on, especially once you start to notice the benefits.

SUNDAY

Type of Meditation	*A body scan meditation (app: Insight Timer)*
Duration	*10 minutes*
Daily Mindfulness Practices	*Making tea* *Cleaning teeth*
Observations and Notes	*I felt irritable when I meditated but I stayed with the practice …* *I meditated lying down and fell asleep during part of it.* *I found it hard to stay with the process of making tea, but I used the time to breathe and felt slightly calmer. It felt like a long time.*
Three Things I am Grateful for Today…	*Grateful for my house, my health and my job.*

MONDAY

Type of Meditation	
Duration	
Daily Mindfulness Practices	
Observations and Notes	
Three Things I am Grateful for Today…	

TUESDAY

Type of Meditation	
Duration	
Daily Mindfulness Practices	
Observations and Notes	
Three Things I am Grateful for Today…	

WEDNESDAY

Type of Meditation	
Duration	
Daily Mindfulness Practices	
Observations and Notes	
Three Things I am Grateful for Today…	

THURSDAY

Type of Meditation	
Duration	
Daily Mindfulness Practices	
Observations and Notes	
Three Things I am Grateful for Today...	

FRIDAY

Type of Meditation	
Duration	
Daily Mindfulness Practices	
Observations and Notes	
Three Things I am Grateful for Today...	

SATURDAY

Type of Meditation	
Duration	
Daily Mindfulness Practices	
Observations and Notes	
Three Things I am Grateful for Today…	

SUNDAY

Type of Meditation	
Duration	
Daily Mindfulness Practices	
Observations and Notes	
Three Things I am Grateful for Today…	

MONDAY

Type of Meditation	
Duration	
Daily Mindfulness Practices	
Observations and Notes	
Three Things I am Grateful for Today...	

TUESDAY

Type of Meditation	
Duration	
Daily Mindfulness Practices	
Observations and Notes	
Three Things I am Grateful for Today...	

WEDNESDAY

Type of Meditation	
Duration	
Daily Mindfulness Practices	
Observations and Notes	
Three Things I am Grateful for Today...	

THURSDAY

Type of Meditation	
Duration	
Daily Mindfulness Practices	
Observations and Notes	
Three Things I am Grateful for Today...	

FRIDAY

Type of Meditation	
Duration	
Daily Mindfulness Practices	
Observations and Notes	
Three Things I am Grateful for Today…	

SATURDAY

Type of Meditation	
Duration	
Daily Mindfulness Practices	
Observations and Notes	
Three Things I am Grateful for Today…	

SUNDAY

Type of Meditation	
Duration	
Daily Mindfulness Practices	
Observations and Notes	
Three Things I am Grateful for Today…	

ENDNOTES

1. Killingsworth, M, and Gilbert, D, 'A Wandering Mind is an Unhappy Mind', 330 SCIENCE 932 (Nov 2010).

2. Basso, J C, McHale, A, Ende, V, Oberlin, D J, and Suzuki, W A (2018). Brief, daily meditation enhances attention, memory, mood, and emotional regulation in non-experienced meditators. Behavioural Brain Research. See also Goleman, D, and Davidson, R, *The Science of Meditation: How to Change Your Brain, Mind and Body*, Penguin Life, 2018, p21.

3. Mrazek, M D, et al, 'Mindfulness and Mind Wandering: Finding Convergence Through Opposing Constructs', *Emotion*, 12:3 (2012); 442-48.

4. Wood, A M, Joseph, S, Lloyds, J, Atkins, S, 'Gratitude Influences Sleep Through The Mechanism of Pre-Sleep Cognitions', *Journal of Psychosomatic Research* 66 (2009), 43–48.

5. This claim was made by the Laboratory of Neuroimaging (LONI) at the University of Southern California, with caveats: 'This is still an open question (how many thoughts does the average human brain process in one day). LONI faculty have

done some very preliminary studies using undergraduate student volunteers and have estimated that one may expect around 60–70K thoughts per day. These results are not peer-reviewed or published. There is no generally accepted definition of what "thought" is or how it is created. *In our study, we had assumed that a "thought" is a sporadic single-idea cognitive concept resulting from the act of thinking, or produced by spontaneous systems-level cognitive brain activations.*' See the reference to 'Approximately 70,000' at:

http://ccb.loni.usc.edu/training/neurology-fun-facts-quiz-answer-key/

The comments made by LONI were reported by The Neurocritic website:

https://neurocritic.blogspot.com/2015/09/neurohackers-gone-wild.html

---

6. **Attention:** Verhaegen P, *Presence: How Mindfulness And Meditation Shape Your Brain, Mind and Life*, at p.96, Oxford University Press, 2017. One comprehensive review of mindfulness research concluded that the average meditator had stronger attention skills than 72 per cent of non-meditators. See also Tang, Y, et al, 'Short-Term Meditation Training Improves Attention and Self-Regulation', Proceedings of the National Academy of Sciences of the United States of America, 2007:

http://www.pnas.org/content/104/43/17152.short

See also the work of Amishi P Jha who found that novices trained in MBSR (Mindfulness Based Stress Reduction) significantly improved in orienting, a component of selective attention that directs the mind to target one among an infinite array of sensory inputs: Jha, A, Krompinger, J, and Baime, M J (2007). 'Mindfulness Training Modifies Subsystems of Attention.' *Cognitive Affective and Behavioral Neuroscience*, 7, 109–119, available at:

http://www.amishi.com/lab/assets/pdf/2007_JhaKrompingerBaime.pdf.

Decision-making: Jha, A, 'Being in the Now', 24(1) *Scientific American Mind* 26–33 (Mar/Apr 2013); Ricard, M, Lutz, A, and Davidson, R, 'Mind of the Mediator', 311(5) *Scientific American*, 38–45 (Nov 2014). See also Kerelaia, N, and Reb, J (2014). 'Improving Decision Making Through Mindfulness – A Working Paper'. Insead. Retrieved from:

http://sites.insead.edu/facultyresearch/research/doc.cfm?did=54608

Working memory: In their book *The Distracted Mind*, Gazzaley and Rosen describe working memory as an element of cognitive control, which allows you to 'hold information actively in the mind for brief periods of time to guide our subsequent actions. It is essential to everyday functioning and forms connections throughout our day that are transient and usually take place without our conscious awareness.' Gazzaley, A and Rosen, L D, *The Distracted Mind – Ancient Brains in a High-Tech World*, MIT Press, 2016. The average effect over five studies on working memory showed that the average meditator has a better working memory than 62 per cent of non-meditators. See Verhaeghen, P, *Presence, How Mindfulness and Meditation Shape Your Brain, Mind and Life*, p.111, footnote 54, citing Banks et al (2015), Chambers et al (2008), Jha et al (2010), Morrison et al (2013), Mrazek et al (2013).

Stress reduction: See 'Mindfulness-Based Stress Reduction for Stress Management in Healthy People: a Review and Meta-analysis'. Chiesa, A, Serretti, A, J Altern, *Journal of Alternative and Complementary Medicine*, 2009 May;15 (5):593–600. doi: 10.1089/acm.2008.0495. See also: 'Mindfulness-Based Stress Reduction as a Stress Management Intervention for Healthy Individuals: A Systematic Review', *Journal of Evidence-Based Complementary and Alternative Medicine 194, July 2014.*

Immune system: Researchers from the University of Wisconsin-Madison investigated the effects of mindfulness on the immune system response whereby they injected participants with a flu virus at the end of an eight-week course. They found that the mindfulness group had a significantly stronger immune system compared to the others. See 'Alterations in Brain and Immune Function Produced by Mindfulness Meditation', Davidson, R J, Kabat-Zinn, J, Schumacher, J, Rosenkranz, M, Muller, D, Santorelli, S F, Urbanowski, F, Harrington, A, Bonus K, Sheridan, J F, *Psychosom Med*, 2003 Jul–Aug; 65(4): 564–70.

Anxiety and depression: In 2016, in the most comprehensive scientific review of its kind, The Oxford Mindfulness Centre found that Mindfulness-Based Cognitive Behavioural Therapy (MBCT) appears to be efficient as a 'treatment for relapse prevention for those with recurrent depression, particularly those with more pronounced symptoms.' The practice of MBCT teaches you how to pay closer attention to the present moment and let go of the negative thoughts and ruminations that can trigger depression. Patients who engaged in the therapy were 23 per cent less likely to suffer an episode of relapse than those who didn't, even if they stopped taking their antidepressants. MBCT helps people to inquire into, familiarise themselves with, and redirect the thought process that is getting them into trouble (eg negative self-talk). They learn to identify stress and signs of depression before a crisis hits. See also: Kuyken, W, Warren, F C, Taylor, R S, et al, Efficacy of Mindfulness-Based Cognitive Therapy in Prevention of Depressive Relapse: An Individual Patient Data Meta-analysis From Randomised Trials. *JAMA Psychiatry.*2016;73(6):565–574. doi:10.1001/jamapsychiatry.2016.0076.

See two articles on this subject: 'Mindfulness-Based Cognitive Therapy May Reduce Recurrent Depression Risk' by Catherine Crane and Zindel Segal, 24 May 2016:

https://www.mindful.org/mindfulness-based-cognitive-therapy-recurrent-depression/.

See also Mindfulness for Anxiety: Research and Practice', 16 February 2017:

https://www.mindful.org/mindfulness-for-anxiety-research-and-practice/

See also the randomised studies carried out in 2000: Teasdale, J D, Williams, M G, Soulsby, J M, Segal, Z V, Ridgeway, V V, Lau, M A, 'Prevention of Relapse/Recurrence in Major Depression' by Mindfulness-Based Cognitive Therapy, *Journal of Consulting and Clinical Psychology*, 2000, vol 68, no 4, 615–623. See also the randomised trial carried out in 2008: Kuyken, W, Byford, S, Taylor, R S, et al, 'Mindfulness-Based Cognitive Therapy to Prevent Relapse in Recurrent Depression'. *Journal of Consulting and Clinical Psychology* 2008; 76(6): 966–978.

ADHD: In a study of fifty adult ADHD patients, the group that was submitted to MBCT (Mindfulness-Based Cognitive Therapy) demonstrated reduced hyperactivity, reduced impulsivity and increased 'act-with-awareness' skill, contributing to an overall improvement in inattention symptoms: *Clinical Neurophysiology*: 'Effects of Mindfulness-Based Cognitive Therapy on Neurophysiological Correlates of Performance Monitoring in Adult Attention-Deficit/Hyperactivity Disorder,' July 2014, vol 125, issue 7, pp1407–1416.

Insomnia: 'Mindfulness Meditation and Improvement in Sleep Quality and Daytime Impairment Among Older Adults with Sleep Disturbances', David S Black et al; 'Mindfulness Meditation and Improvement in Sleep Quality and Daytime Impairment Among Older Adults with Sleep Disturbances: A Randomised Clinical Trial', Black, D S, O'Reilly, G A, Olmstead, R, Breen, E C, Irwin, M R, *JAMA Intern Med.* 2015 Apr; 175(4): 494–501. See also: 'A Low Dose Mindfulness Intervention and Recovery from Work: Effects on Psychological Detachment, Sleep Quality, and Sleep Duration', Hülsheger U R, Feinholdt A, Nubold A, *Journal of Occupational and Organizational Psychology, vol 88, issue 3.*

7.   Case Study: Depression and Anxiety: Fuchs, C H, et al:
     'Implementation of an Acceptance-and Mindfulness-Based Group
     for Depression and Anxiety in Primary Care: Initial Outcomes',
     Fuchs, C H, et al, Families, Systems & Health: *The Journal of
     Collaborative Family Healthcare*, vol 34, no 4, 2016, pp386–395.

8.   Wellbeing at the Bar – A Resilience Framework Assessment by
     Positive, April 2015, available at:

     https://www.barcouncil.org.uk/media/348371/wellbeing_at_the_bar_
     report_april_2015__final_.pdf

9.   Resilience and Wellbeing Survey Report, The Law Society, April
     2018, available at:

     http://communities.lawsociety.org.uk/Uploads/p/d/i/jld-resilience-and-
     wellbeing-survey-report-2018.pdf

10. Krill, P, Johnson, R and Albert, L, 'The Prevalence of
     Substance Use and Other Mental Health Concerns Among
     American Attorneys', 10. ADDICT. MED. 46, 48-51 (2016),
     available at:

     https://journals.lww.com/journaladdictionmedicine/fulltext/2016/02000/
     The_Prevalence_of_Substance_Use_and_Other_Mental.8.aspx

11. See National Task Force on Lawyer Well-Being, 'The Path to
     Lawyer Well-Being: Practical Recommendations for Positive
     Change' (Aug 2017), p1, available at:

     https://www.americanbar.org/content/dam/aba/images/abanews/The
     PathToLawyerWellBeingReportRevFINAL.pdf

12. In research carried out by Barnado's and YouGov, 79 per cent of social workers who participated in a survey stated that statutory sector workers were stressed, with many experiencing long-term sickness as a result, available at:

https://www.communitycare.co.uk/2018/10/04/cuts-stress-long-term-sickness-social-workers/

In a YouGov survey conducted in 2018 among 911 teachers in Great Britain, 83 per cent of those who participated stated that they feel stressed as a result of their job. The most common cause of their stress was workload, reported by 60 per cent of those participating. The report is available at:

https://yougov.co.uk/topics/economy/articles-reports/2018/11/29/teachers-stressed-and-undervalued-satisfied-their-

A survey by the British Medical Association in 2017 indicated that 50% of the 422 doctors who responded reported feeling unwell due to work-related stress during the previous year. More than six out of ten respondents (61%) felt their stress levels had increased during this period, while only 6% indicated they had reduced: BMA Quarterly Tracker Survey - Q2. BMA Surv. 2017;(2).

---

13. Paulsen, B, 'Make Peace With Your Anxious Brain', *Mindful*, April 2019. The article explains that 'The neuroscientist whose work led to the realisation that anxiety arises from two distinct neural pathways is Joseph LeDoux.'

---

14. Case Study: The Young Brain: Luders, E, et al, 'Estimating Brain Age Using High Resolution Pattern Recognition: Younger

Brains in Long-Term Meditation Practitioners', Neuro-image (2016).

15. Gazzaley, A, and Rosen, L D, 'The Distracted Mind', The MIT Press, 2016, p15.

16. Ibid, at p11.

17. The Communications Market 2018, Ofcom, available at:

   https://www.ofcom.org.uk/research-and-data/multi-sector-research/cmr/cmr-2018

18. Gazzaley, A and Rosen, L D, 'The Distracted Mind', The MIT Press, 2016, p120, footnote 50.

19. Lanaj, K, Johnson, R E, and Barnes, C M, 'Beginning the Workday yet Already Depleted? Consequences of Late-Night Smartphone Use and Sleep', *Organizational Behavior and Human Decision Processes* 124, no 1 (2014): 11–23.

20. Case Study: Distraction: Marulanda-Carter, L, Jackson, T W, 'Effects of E-mail Addiction and Interruptions on Employees', *Journal of Systems and Information Technology 14*, no 1 (2012): 82–94.

21. Verhaegen, P, *Presence: How Mindfulness And Meditation Shape Your Brain, Mind and Life*, at p.96, Oxford University Press, 2017.

22. Case Study: Improvements to Attention: 'Cognitive Aging and Long-Term Maintenance of Attentional Improvements Following Meditation Training', Zanesco, A P, King, B G, MacLean, K A, et al, *Journal of Cognitive Enhancement* (2018) 2: 259.

23. Thornton B, Faires A, Robbins M and Rollins E, 'The Mere Presence of a Cell Phone May Be Distracting: Implications for Attention and Task Performance', *Social Psychology*, 45 (2014): 479–488.

24. Thich Nhat Hanh on Walking Meditation, 5 April 2018, available at:

https://www.lionsroar.com/how-to-meditate-thich-nhat-hanh-on-walking-meditation/

25. Case Study: Reducing Anxiety: 'Three-Year Follow-Up and Clinical Implications of a Mindfulness Meditation-Based Stress Reduction Intervention in the Treatment of Anxiety Disorders', Miller, J J, Fletcher, K, Kabat-Zinn, J, *General Hospital Psychiatry* 17, (3) (05): 192–200.

26. Brach, T, 'The Trance of Fear', 24 July 2013, available at:

https://www.tarabrach.com/the-trance-of-fear/

See also Brach, T, *Radical Acceptance – Awakening The Love That Heals Fear and Shame Within Us*, Tara Brach, 2003.

27. Ibid.

28. Extract taken from the poem 'Community of the Spirit' by Rumi.

29. Gathering the Evidence Base for Mindfulness at Work: Scientifically Evaluated and Academic Research (2016). Retrieved from:

    http://www.mindfulnet.org/page18.htm

    Glomb, T M, Duffy, M K, Bono, J E, and Yang, T (2011). 'Mindfulness at Work.' *Personnel and Human Resources Management*, 30, 115–157. See also Kerelaia, N & Reb J (2014. 'Improving Decision Making Through Mindfulness – A Working Paper'. Insead. Retrieved from:

    http://sites.insead.edu/facultyresearch/research/doc.cfm?did=54608

30. Ophir, E, Nass, C, Wagner, A D, 'Cognitive Control in Media Multi-Taskers', Proceedings of the National Academy of Sciences, September 2009, 106 (37) 15583–15587.

31. Boris Cyrulnik, Resilience – *How Your Inner Strength Can Set You Free From The Past*, p.51. Boris Cyrulnik was born in 1937. In 1942 his parents were deported to a concentration camp and never returned. Maltreated by his foster parents, he was eventually chosen as a runner in the liberation, perilously crossing enemy lines to deliver messages to French fighters. He was seven. This personal trauma helped to develop his belief that trauma is not destiny.

32. Wu, Gang, Feder, A, Cohen, H, Kim, J J, Calderon, S, Charney, D S, Mather, A A, 'Understanding Resilience', *Frontiers in Behavioral Neuroscience*, 15 February 2013. Epigenetics is the study of biological mechanisms that switch genes on and off. See:

    https://www.whatisepigenetics.com/what-is-epigenetics/

33. Rutter, M (2012). 'Resilience as a Dynamic Concept'. *Development and Psychopathology*, 24(2), 335–344.

---

34. 'Growing Resilience: An Interview with Dr Rick Hanson', 12 April 2018, available at:

https://www.goodtherapy.org/blog/growing-resilience-interview-dr-rick-hanson-0412185

---

35. Bajaj, B, and Pande, N, 'Mediating Role of Resilience in the Impact of Mindfulness on Life Satisfaction and Effect as Indices of Subjective Well-being, Personality and Individual Differences', vol 93, April 2016, pages 63–67.

---

36. Keye, M D, Pidgeon A M, 'An Investigation of the Relationship between Resilience, Mindfulness, and Academic Self-Efficacy', *Open Journal of Social Sciences*, 2013, vol 1, no 6, 1–4, available at:

https://pdfs.semanticscholar.org/6ca6/efd335d147bdd0a0a9580f0cfd59a273367c.pdf

See also the work of Jha, A P, Stanley, E A, Kiyonaga, A, Wong, L, and Gelfand, L (2010). 'Examining the Protective Effects of Mindfulness Training on Working Memory and Affective Experience', *Emotion* 64–54 ,(1)10, available at:

http://www.amishi.com/lab/wp-content/uploads/jha_stanley_etal_emotion_2010.pdf

See also Jha, A P, Krompinger, J, and Baime, M J (2007), 'Mindfulness Training Modifies Subsystems of Attention',

Cognitive Affective and Behavioral Neuroscience, 7, 109-119, available at:

http://www.amishi.com/lab/assets/pdf/2007_JhaKrompingerBaime.pdf

37. 'Sleep Matters: The Impact of Sleep on Health and Wellbeing', Mental Health Awareness Week, 2011, available at:

https://www.mentalhealth.org.uk/sites/default/files/MHF-Sleep-Report-2011.pdf

38. Killgore, W, 'Effects of Sleep Deprivation on Cognition. Progress in Brain Research', 185. 105–29, available at:

www.researchgate.net/publication/47790667_Effects_of_sleep_deprivation_on_cognition

39. Shockey, T M, Wheaton, A G, Short Sleep Duration by Occupation Group – 29 states, 2013–2014, Centers for Disease Control and Prevention, 2 March 2017, 66(8); 207–213.

40. 'How Sleep Deprivation is Affecting UK Workers', 7 November 2017, available at:

https://www.cv-library.co.uk/recruitment-insight/effects-sleep-deprivation-workplace/

41. 'Why Sleep Matters: Quantifying the Economic Costs of Insufficient Sleep', Rand Corporation, available at:

https://www.rand.org/randeurope/research/projects/the-value-of-the-sleep-economy.html

42. Black, D S, O'Reilly, G A, Olmstead, R, Breen, E C, Irwin, M R, 'Mindfulness Meditation and Improvement in Sleep Quality and Daytime Impairment Among Older Adults With Sleep Disturbances', A Randomised Clinical Trial, *JAMA* Intern Med, April, 2015; 175(4); 494–501, available at:

https://www.ncbi.nlm.nih.gov/pmc/articles/PMC4407465/

43. Ong, J C, Manber, R, Segal, Z, Xia, Y, Shapiro, S, Wyatt, J K, 'A Randomised Controlled Trial of Mindfulness Meditation for Chronic Insomnia, Sleep.' 2014 Sep 1; 37(9): 1553–63. Available at:

https://www.ncbi.nlm.nih.gov/pubmed/25142566

44. Case Study: Improving Sleep, Hülsheger, U R, Feinholdt, A, Nübold, A, 'A Low-Dose Mindfulness Intervention and Recovery From Work: Effects on Psychological Detachment, Sleep Quality, and Sleep Duration', *Journal of Occupational and Organizational Psychology*, vol 88, issue 3, 22 March 2015.

In this study, researchers found that after eight weeks, those who took part in the meditation training had less total wake time during the night, were more relaxed before going to bed, and reduced the severity of their sleep problems. In a follow-up study six months later, the insomnia sufferers had maintained a better quality of sleep.

45. Case Study: Loving Kindness: Hutcherson, C A, et al, 'Loving Kindness Meditation Increases Social Connectedness', *Emotion* 8:5 (2008): 720–24.

46. Neff, K, Germer, C, *The Mindful Self-Compassion Workbook, A Proven Way to Accept Yourself, Build Inner Strength and Thrive*, Guilford Press, 2018, pp10–11. In her article 'Self-Compassion and Psychological Well-Being', Kristen Neff explains that 'Over-identification is a process in which your sense of self becomes so immersed in subjective emotional reactions that you are carried away by your emotions, which tend to become exaggerated as a result.' – *Constructivism in the Human Sciences*, vol 9 (2), 2004, p27–37 at p29.

47. 'Kind to Me' by Kristen Neff and Christopher Germer, *Mindful*, February 2019, p45.

48. Neff, K D, Germer, C, 'The Transformative Effects of Mindful Self-Compassion', 29 January 2019, available at:

https://www.mindful.org/the-transformative-effects-of-mindful-self-compassion/

49. Neff, K D, 'The Role of Self-Compassion in Development: A Healthier Way to Relate to Oneself, Human Development', 2009; 52: 211–214. Most of the research studies on self-compassion in recent years have relied on individuals self-reporting their experience. See Neff, K D (2003) – 'Development and Validation of a Scale to Measure Self-Compassion', *Self and Identity*, 2, 223–250.

50. Singer, T, Klimecki, O, 'Empathy and Compassion', *Current Biology*, 24:15 (2014). Weng et al, 'Compassion Training Alters Altruism and Neural Responses to Suffering', 2013.

51. Fredrickson, B L, Cohn, M A, Coffey, K A, Pek, J and Finkel, S M (2008). 'Open Hearts Build Lives: Positive Emotions, InducedThrough Loving-Kindness Meditation, Build Consequential Personal Resources'. *Journal of personality and social psychology*, 95(5), 1045–1062.

---

52. Shahar, B, Szsepsenwol, O, Zilcha-Mano, S, Haim, N, Zamir, O, Levi-Yeshuvi, S, Levit-Binnun, N, 'A Wait-List Randomised Controlled Trial of Loving-Kindness Meditation Programme for Self-Criticism', *Clinical Psychology & Psychother*, 2015, Jul–Aug; 22(4): 346–56, available at:

https://www.ncbi.nlm.nih.gov/pubmed/24633992

---

53. Case Study: Working Memory: Verhaeghen, P, *Presence: How Mindfulness and Meditation Shape Your Brain, Mind and Life*, Oxford University Press, 2017. The author refers at p.111 to five studies on working memory:

Banks, J B, Welhaf, M S, Srour, A, 'The Protective Effects of Brief Mindfulness Meditation Training, *Consciousness and Cognition*', vol 33, May 2015, pp.277–285.

Chambers, R, Chuen Yee Lo, B, Allen, N B, 'The Impact of Intensive Mindfulness Training on Attentional Control, Cognitive Style, and Affect', *Cognitive Therapy and Research* (2008) 32:303–322.

Jha, A P, Stanley E A, Kiyonaga, A, Wong, L, and Gelfand, L (2010). 'Examining the Protective Effects of Mindfulness Training on Working Memory and Affective Experience'. *Emotion*,(1)10

64–54. Morrison A B, Goolsarran M, Rogers S L, and Jha A P (2014). 'Taming a Wandering Attention: Short-Form Mindfulness Training in Student Cohorts', *Frontiers in Human Neuroscience*, 7, 897.

Mrazek, M D, Franklin, M S, Phillips, D T, Baird, B, Schooler, J W, 'Mindfulness Training Improves Working Memory Capacity and GRE Performance While Reducing Mind Wandering', *Psychol Sci* 2013, May, 24(5); 776–81.

54. Mehrabian, A, '*Silent Messages: Implicit Communication of Emotions and Attitudes*', Wadsworth Publishing Co Inc, 1981.

55. TED Talks: 'A Simple Way to Break a Bad Habit', 24 February 2016, available at:

https://www.youtube.com/watch?v=-moW9jvvMr4

See also, Brewer, J, '*A Simple Way to Break a Bad Habit*', *Mindful Magazine*, 10 November 2017, available at: https://www.mindful.org/simple-way-break-bad-habit/

56. The acronym RAIN was first coined by Michele McDonald. For an article by Jack Kornfield on how to apply the RAIN practice, see this article:

www.lionsroar.com/how-rain-can-nourish-you/

RESOURCES

GUIDED MEDITATIONS

The guided meditations at the end of each chapter are available for download from the Practical Meditation website at www.practicalmeditation.co.uk/podcasts

WEBSITES

Mindful: www.mindful.org

Practical Meditation: www.practicalmeditation.co.uk

The American Mindfulness Research Association (AMRA):

https://goamra.org

The Center for Compassion and Altruism Research and Education: ccare.stanford.edu

The Center For Mindfulness at the University of Massachusetts Medical School: www.umassmed.edu/cfm

The Greater Good Science Center, Berkeley University:

https://greatergood.berkeley.edu

Wild Mind: www.wildmind.org

BOOKS

Benson, H, and Proctor, W, *Relaxation Revolution: The Science and Genetics of Mind and Body Healing*, Scribner, 2010

Benson, H, *The Relaxation Response*, Avon Books, 2000

Brach, T, *Radical Acceptance: Awakening The Love That Heals Fear and Shame Within Us*, Rider, 2003

Brantley, J, *Calming Your Anxious Mind: How Mindfulness and Compassion Can Free You From Anxiety, Fear and Panic*, New Harbinger Publications, 2nd edition, 2007

Brown, B, *Braving the Wildnerness: The Quest for True Belonging and the Courage to Stand Alone*, Random House, 2017

Burch, V and Irvin, C, *Mindfulness for Women: Declutter Your Mind, Simplify Your Life, Find Time to 'Be'*, Piatkus, 2016

Chödrön, P, *Living Beautifully With Uncertainty and Change*, Shambhala Publications Inc, 2012

Chödrön, P, *The Wisdom of No Escape: How To Love Yourself and Your World*, Element Books, New Edition, 2004

Chödrön, P, *When Things Fall Apart: Heart Advice For Difficult Times*, Shambhala Publications Inc, 1997

Cyrulnik, B, *Resilience: How Your Inner Strength Can Set You Free From The Past*, Tarcherperigee Original Edition, 2009

Daisley, B, *The Joy of Work: 30 Ways To Fix Your Work Culture and Fall in Love With Your Job Again*, Random House Business, 2019

Emmons, R A, *Thanks!: How the New Science of Gratitude Can Make You Happier*, Houghton Miffin Annotated Edition, 2007

Ford, A, *Seeking Silence in a Noisy World*, Ivy Press, 2010

Frankl, VE, *Man's Search for Meaning*, Washington Square Press, 1959

Gazzaley, A, and Rosen, L D, *The Distracted Mind*, MIT Press, 2016

Goleman, D, and Davidson, R, *The Science of Meditation: How to Change Your Brain, Mind and Body*, Penguin Life 2nd Edition, 2018

Hall, J, *Breathe: Simple Breathing Techniques for a Calmer, Happier Life*, Quadrille Publishing, 2016

Hamilton, D R, *Why Kindness is Good For You*, Hay House UK, 2010

Hamilton, D R, *It's The Thought That Counts: The Astonishing Evidence of the Power of the Mind over Matter*, Hay House UK, 2005

Hanh, T N, *The Miracle of Mindfulness: The Classic Guide*, Rider Classic Edition, 1975

Hanh, T N, *How to Eat*, Parallex Press, 2014

Hanh, T N, *Fear – Essential Wisdom For Getting Through The Storm*, Rider, 2012

Hanh, T N, *Peace is Every Step: The Path of Mindfulness in Everyday Life*, Rider, 1991

Hanh, T N, *The Miracle of Mindfulness: Manual on Meditation*, Beacon Press, 1995

Hanh, T N, *No Mud, No Lotus: The Art of Transforming Suffering*, Parallex Press, p122, 2014

Hanh, T N, *Silence: The Power of Quiet in a World Full of Noise*, HarperOne, 2015

Hanson, R, *Hardwiring Happiness: The Practical Science of Reshaping Your Brain – and Your Life*, Harmony, 2013

Harrison, E, *Teach Yourself to Meditate: Over 20 Simple Exercises for Peace, Health and Clarity of Mind*, Piatkus New Edition, 1993

Hasson, G, *Mindfulness Pocketbook: Little Exercises for a Calmer Life*, John Wiley & Sons Ltd, 2015

Hawn, G, Holden, W, *10 Mindful Minutes: Giving Our Children – and Ourselves – The Social and Emotional Skills to Reduce Stress and Anxiety for Healthier, Happier Lives*, Piatkus, 2011

Kabat-Zinn, J, *Wherever you Go, There You Are: Mindfulness Meditation in Everyday Life*, Piatkus New Edition, 2004

Kabat-Zinn, J, *Full Catastrophe Living: Using the Wisdom of Your Body and Mind to Face Stress, Pain and Illness*, Penguin Random House USA, 1990

Kagge, E, *Silence In The Age of Noise*, Viking, 2017

Kornfield, J, *The Wise Heart*, Rider, 2008

Marchant, D, *Pause Every Day: 20 Mindful Practices for Calm & Clarity*, Aster, 2018

Mogi, K, *The Little Book of Ikigai*, Quercus, 2017

Neff, K, Germer, C, *The Mindful Self-Compassion Workbook, A Proven Way to Accept Yourself, Build Inner Strength and Thrive*, Guilford Press, 2018

Nepo, M, *Seven Thousand Ways to Listen*, Aria Books, 2012

Nepo, M, *The Book of Awakening: Having the Life You Want by Being Present to the Life You Have*, Conari Press, 2000

O'Morain, P, *Mindfulness for Worriers,* Yellow Kite, 2015

Pearson, M, *Meditation: The Stress Solution,* Hothive Books, 2011

Rinpoche, S, *The Tibetan Book of Living and Dying* Rider, New Edition, 1998

Salzberg, S, *Loving Kindness. The Revolutionary Art of Happiness,* Shambhala Publications Inc, 2004

Salzberg, S, *Real Happiness, A 28-day Programme to Connect with the Power of Meditation,* Hay House UK, 2011

Sinclair, M, and Seydel, J, *Working with Mindfulness: Keeping Calm and Focused to Get the Job Done,* FT Press, 2016

Teasdale, J, Williams, M, and Segal, Z, *The Mindful Way Workbook: An 8-Week Program to Free Yourself From Depression and Emotional Distress,* Guilford Press, 2014

Tolle, E, *The Power of Now: A Guide to Spiritual Enlightenment,* Yellow Kite, 2001

Verhaeghen, P, *Presence: How Mindfulness and Meditation Shape Your Brain, Mind and Life,* OUP USA, 2017

Wax, R, *A Mindfulness Guide for the Frazzled,* Penguin Life, 2016

Wax, R, *Sane New World: Taming the Mind,* Hodder & Stoughton, 2013

Williams, M, and Penman, D, *Mindfulness: A Practical Guide to Finding Peace in a Frantic World,* Piatkus, 2014

Wilson Schaef, A, *Meditations for Women Who Do Too Much,* HarperOne, 1990

ACKNOWLEDGEMENTS

This book would not have been written without the support of my partner Michael. Thank you for your patience, editorial wisdom and kindness. Thank you to my daughter Amelia for inspiring my mindfulness journey. Her reminder to 'breathe' when I got irritated, my parents' support to keep on going, and my nephew's young eagle-eye all contributed to the final product. Thanks also to my brother and sisters-in-law for their support and encouragement. And to my nan for being willing to try mindfulness in her nineties.

The help of my talented friends Michelle, Abi, Miranda and Andrew was also invaluable when reading early drafts and helping me to find my voice.

Thank you to Barbara, my first mindfulness teacher, for her grace, insight and inspiration. I am also grateful to Mary and Christa from The British School of Meditation and to Terry, for reminding me that if I wanted to write, I had to set a deadline and simply get on with it. I would also like to thank Catherine Baksi who wrote an article in *The Evening Standard* about my first mindfulness classes at Gray's Inn.

Many thanks to Mark Williams, Sharon Salzberg, Steven Kay QC, Mary Pearson, Carolyn McCombe, Nick Hill, Elizabeth Rimmer and David McCahon for reading and reviewing early drafts of the book. I am also grateful to the support I have received from 9 Bedford Row, Gray's Inn and The Bar Council.

Thank you finally to Heather Boisseau, Clare Christian and their team at RedDoor Press. Your help has been invaluable in bringing this book to life.

ABOUT THE AUTHOR

Gillian Higgins is an international criminal barrister and commercial mediator at The Chambers of 9 Bedford Row, in London. Over the past twenty years, she has represented leading political figures  in trials of genocide, crimes against humanity and war crimes before the International Criminal Court and the United Nations international criminal tribunals in The Hague and Tanzania.

Gillian is also a mindfulness meditation teacher and is actively involved in promoting well-being in the legal profession. She has pioneered the introduction of mindfulness at the Bar and teaches professionals in the workplace and members of her community at home.

Gillian lives in West Sussex with her partner and daughter.

Find out more about RedDoor Press and sign up to our newsletter to hear about our **latest releases, author events,** exciting **competitions** and more at

reddoorpress.co.uk

YOU CAN ALSO FOLLOW US:

  @RedDoorBooks

  Facebook.com/RedDoorPress

  @RedDoorBooks